HOW TO ENCOUNTER THE

L O V E

OF *God*

DR. PATTY SADALLAH

HOW TO ENCOUNTER THE

L O V E

OF *God*

DR. PATTY SADALLAH

Dedication

To Maureen

My heaven-sent messenger who introduced me

to the LOVE of God.

Table of Contents

Acknowledgements

My sincere thanks go out to the faithful people who participated in the LOVE book class and Spirit Life Circle Mentors who agreed to share their encounter stories and comments in this book: Roma Flood, George Medellin, Monica Hoffmann, Chris Lewicki, Mike Bastien, Cindy Fiebig, Jacqueline Puliafico. Hannah Chen and Charisse Anderson. And thanks to Dr Isabelle Knockaert Declerq for sharing her dissertation insights.

I would like to thank my daughter Jamael Szucs and Larry Silver for their careful editing. And my husband George and other daughters Leah and Noelle for their constant support. A special thanks to my sister, Michele McLaughlin, who is my biggest fan and gives my books away freely to everyone she meets!

Thanks to Julie Sordi who made the beautiful lyric video collages for each chapter and to Tasha Markovich my wonderful collage photographer. And to each and every artist for whom we were blessed by their inspirational songs: Lauren Daigle, Colton Dixon, David Dunn, David Crowder Band, Tenth Avenue North, Unspoken and Love and the Outcome.

11

Thank you Matias Baldanza the book cover designer, Daiana Morales the paperback and E-Book formatter. Thank you to Kathy Jiamboi and Kristen Rosenstock from Creative Edge Marketing for the gift of the beautiful series logos.

I'd like to thank my faithful prayer partners Dr. Anthony Raimondo, Larry Silver and Katie Beckwith.

And last but by no means least, I would like to thank Jesus for showing up for each person as all these Names so faithfully!

All media links are found on the Experience Jesus page of PattySadallah.com and are identified by type of media and book page number. Keep this webpage open so you can simply click to the next media link in the book to watch, listen and experience everything without missing a beat! Website:

www.PattySadallah.com/Experience-Jesus.

You've Always Been by Unspoken

https://bit.ly/3kCslLp

Experience Jesus
Series Introduction

God's TV Channel

*I*magine that God has His own TV channel. Just like others you might have at your fingertips. But unlike everything on your TV, His is supernatural. When we watch TV, it is a one-directional experience. You can see and emotionally connect with the programming on other channels as a distant observer. But the God channel is a two-way experience. You jump through the television and become part of God's action. This may seem like a strange idea to you, but essentially, this is the experience you will have with this book series. You will learn how to access God through the eyes and ears of your heart to connect with the various Names of Him directly.

John 10:27 "My sheep hear My voice, and I know them, and they follow Me."

One of the reasons Jesus died for us on the cross was to gain us direct access to the Father so we may know Him intimately one Name at a time.

Colossians 1:9-12 "⁹For this reason also, since the day we heard of it, we have not ceased to pray for you and to ask that you may be filled with the knowledge of His will in all spiritual wisdom and understanding, ¹⁰so that you will walk in a manner worthy of the LORD, to please Him in all respects, bearing fruit in every good work and increasing in the knowledge of God; ¹¹strengthened with all power, according to His glorious might, for the attaining of all steadfastness and patience; joyously ¹²giving thanks to the Father, who has qualified us to share in the inheritance of the saints in Light."

This book will guide you to experience Jesus yourself. Together, you will address your personal worries, health, family, future and other life issues. Your experiences with God will move you beyond your limiting beliefs and you will learn how to align yourself with His perfect will for your life.

Why God's Names

The Names of God are personal and powerful. Names like Bridegroom, Mighty Counselor, Friend, Defender, Supernatural Provider, and Healer are intimate for a reason. Would you marry, seek counseling, trust with your secrets or your health, lean on in times of crisis someone you can't see, hear, or feel? God was called these Names because He personally showed up for people in these ways in the days of the Bible. He is even more able to do that for you today!

While researching my last book, I was astonished that the original manuscripts of the Bible contain 955 Names of God. This reference will help you see them in their scriptural contexts. https://bit.ly/313CAiR

Unfortunately, in our English Bible translations, we don't see all these distinctive Names because the English language does not have words to make those distinctions. But they exist, in the Greek, Hebrew, Aramaic, and Latin texts.

In Bible times, people encountered God in a variety of different ways, and then named Him for those experiences. Here is an example from the Bible when Hagar met God personally and gave Him a Name.

> Genesis 16:11-13 (NOG) [11] Then the Messenger of Yahweh said to her, "You are pregnant, and you will give birth to a son. You will name him Ishmael [God Hears], because Yahweh has heard your cry of distress.
>
> [12] He will be as free and wild as an untamed donkey. He will fight with everyone, and everyone will fight with him. He will have conflicts with all his relatives." [a]
>
> [13] Hagar named Yahweh, who had been speaking to her, "You Are **El Roi**." She said, "This is the place where I watched the one who watches over me."

The "Messenger of Yahweh" was the pre-incarnate Jesus. Anytime you see the word *"the"* before the word "angel" of the Lord, or in this translation, "messenger," it is referencing the pre-incarnate Jesus. Hagar knew that she was personally encountering God. She named Him *El Roi.* **El** is another word for Yahweh, which means the complete fullness of God.. She added the word **Roi** to mean "the God who sees me and watches over me." Hagar had met the Omnipresence of God in a personal way.

It was because she experienced what God did for her that she gave Him this Name. Early in my doctoral journey, the Lord helped me understand more about the importance of encountering God's Names. [i]

Knowing about vs. Knowing[1]

I was meditating on a verse in Titus about the notion of people claiming to know God, but it not showing in their behavior.

> Titus 1:16a, They claim to know God, but by their actions they deny Him.

I asked Jesus to show me the difference between someone who thinks they know You and someone who really knows You. (Note that Jesus' voice will always appear indented and in *italics* so it can be easily identified.)

> *The difference is one knows **about** Me, and the other **knows Me intimately**. Let Me show you what I mean.*

Jesus showed me a man in the desert. He had chapped lips and a distressed look on his face. He frantically looked and thought he saw water. But as he kept walking, he realized that it was only a mirage.

---

1 Excerpt from Just ask Jesus Book 1 Series Introduction of How to Live a Worry-Free Life by Dr. Patty Sadallah, pp. 26-28.

There was no real water, only something that looked like water. It's good to know what water looks like. It's better to be able to drink some when you are thirsty!

*To learn about Me is like showing a hungry and thirsty man a picture of a magnificent banquet but there is nothing to eat or drink. Seeing the picture may bring some benefits, but he is left ultimately unsatisfied. The actual need is unfulfilled. This is what it is like to only learn **about** Me.*

*The spiritual need to **know** Me is even stronger than that man's physical need for water. A mirage is an illusion; a trick of the eye caused by light refraction and heat waves. Knowing only about Me is a trick too. But it doesn't fool the soul. The soul knows its need for the True God.*

To truly satisfy the hunger and thirst in your soul, you must drink deeply of the Living Water. Water is refreshing, rejuvenating and restores more than you can see and feel. Come and drink deeply the Living Water. You must eat the food of My Presence. You must enter the Holy of Holies where you can encounter My Presence. I have gained you direct access to the Father by way of the indwelling Holy Spirit by My work on the cross. Do not neglect this privilege.

This is accomplished by you spending time with Me. Consider John 17:3 "This is eternal life, that they may know You, the only true God, and Jesus Christ whom You have sent." To know someone is an intimate thing. To know of something or someone implies knowledge from a distance. It is not My desire for you to know Me distantly or haphazardly in a third-party sort of way as in only through the work of a pastor or a preacher.

You cannot know Me without personally drawing close to Me. It is through steady communion with Me; Father, Son and Holy Spirit that you will truly Know Me. And knowing leads to trusting, believing and obeying which are fruits of the eternal life you now have.

19

It's just like knowing anyone personally. To trust someone, I need to spend time with them to learn who they are and if I can rely on them. After some time, if I feel safe, I tend to want to spend more time and then come to trust them. I spend the most time with people that I like to be around; people who build me up, encourage me and show me love. No one does that better than You, LORD!"

Yes. The difference between knowing in your head and surrendering in your heart is clarified in James 2:19 'You believe that God is one. You do well; the demons also believe, and shudder.' The demons know who I AM, of course. But they do not accept and surrender to Me and have no intimate relationship with Me. This is an important distinction. Remember, I live in your heart, not in your head.

Yes. LORD. I can see the difference.

Every time you take a drink today, spend time reflecting on the Living Water and come and fellowship with Me. Tune to Me in the quiet and listen for My voice. Seek Me and you will find Me. Spend time getting to know Me. Ask Me to show you things. I certainly have a lot to show you! It's My heart's desire to spend time with you too! Communing with Me is the only way for your spiritual hunger and thirst to be satisfied. This is how you truly know Me!

Encountering the Realness of God

I was listening to the dramatized radio version of C.S. Lewis' *The Screwtape Letters*[ii] by Focus on the Family in my car and came to Letter 31. In this last chapter of the book, the Lord grabbed my attention, and I flushed with Glory bumps.

C.S. Lewis wrote the now-classic *Screwtape Letters* in 1942 amidst WWII. It is a fictionalized story that teaches spiritual warfare in reverse. Screwtape is an experienced demon who is counseling his nephew, Wormwood, a new temper assigned to a "patient," much like a guardian angel for the opposite side. Wormwood's job is to speak lies into his patient's ears to keep him away from God's plans and ensure that he stays well below the calling that God (the Enemy as the demons call Him) has for him.

There are 31 letters that Screwtape writes to Wormwood, and each teaches the lies that the enemy speaks into our lives to throw us off our Christian impact. The entire book and dramatized recording are amazing, but what really got my attention was Letter 31!

Here is a list of quoted snippets from this letter that will hopefully shed light on the relevance of what we are doing here in this book series. Screwtape is looking for Wormwood to take him for his punishment for failing with his patient. He goes on a rant about what Wormwood did that lost this patient to the other side for good:

"All our efforts are dismayed...How well I know the instant that they snatched him from us! Did you see it for yourself? ...There was a sudden change in his eyes as he saw you (Wormwood) for the first time, and he recognized the part you had had in him and knew that you had it no longer! ....It was as if he shed for good the all wet clinging garments that held him back and was completely cleansed....

He went so easily! It was sheer instantaneous liberation! Did you mark how, as if he was born for it, the little vermin entered the new life? How all his doubts like in the twinkling of an eye became ridiculous!'...

Do you know what your fatal flaw was? When he saw you, he also saw HIM... You allowed him to see that HE is REAL. ... He, to them, is clarity itself. And worse yet, He was in the form of a MAN! The one for whom he thought was dead

21

is ALIVE and even now at his door! ... All our efforts are dismayed!"[2]

Nothing can stop you when you see Him as **real** and for you now. He is at your door. Meet Him, and you will be free, healed, and transformed into the best version of yourself!

Why we Picture Jesus

The three Persons of the Trinity all play a role in the encountering experience. It is ultimately the **Father** who desires that you commune with Him while seeing and speaking with **Jesus** by the power of the **Holy Spirit.** Jesus is the only person of the Trinity that we can honestly imagine. He was a man like us, and that makes Him accessible and understandable as a person. The Father needs the Perfection of Jesus for us to be able to come near to Him. When the Father looks at you, He sees Jesus covering you with His Perfection. The Power to do this is accomplished by the indwelling Holy Spirit, who is God's very essence inside of every believer. This privilege was accomplished by Jesus's work on the cross.

> Genesis 1:1 (NOG) says [1] In the beginning, **Elohim** created heaven and earth. [2] The earth was formless and empty, and darkness covered the deep water. The **Ruach Elohim** was hovering over the water. [3] Then **Elohim** said, "Let there be light!" So there was light.

Elohim is the plural word for a singular God. You see in this verse that the self-existent **Father God** conceives of the Heavens and the Earth. **Jesus, also called the Word**, speaks this conception into existence, and the **Ruach Elohim**, who is the Holy Spirit is the power that manifests it into reality.

---

2 Focus on the Family Radio Theatre Collector's Edition; The Screwtape Letters by CS Lewis @2009 Tyndale House Publishers. (Snippets from Letter 31)

So, even though you will be connecting with Jesus, know that you are really engaging with Elohim, the Triune God. There will be more on how this works in the Creator Chapter of *How to Encounter the POWER of God: Experience Jesus Book 4.*

Jesus Himself instructs us to encounter the Father God by fixing our eyes on Him. He is the relatable third of the Trinity.

> John 14:7-9 (AMP) [7] If you had [really] known Me, you would also have known My Father. From now on, you know Him and have seen Him."
>
> [8] Philip said to Him, "Lord, show us the Father, and then we will be satisfied." [9] Jesus said to him, "Have I been with you for so long a time, and you do not know Me yet, Philip, nor recognize clearly who I am? Anyone who has seen Me has seen the Father. How can you say, 'Show us the Father?'"

Meet God and Get to Know Yourself

Perhaps one of the most important benefits of the *Experience Jesus* series is that you meet your true self in meeting Him. Referencing the Screwtape Letters again, in one of his earliest letters, Screwtape councils Wormwood that God's strategy is to help people realize that He created them uniquely and distinctly. The Devil's strategy is to have people drift away from their uniquely created selves and become like everyone else. Screwtape shares with Wormwood:

> "When He talks of their losing their selves, He only means abandoning the clamor of self-will; once they have done that, He really gives them back all their personality and boasts (I'm afraid, sincerely) that when they are wholly His, they will be more themselves than ever."[3]

---

3 Focus on the Family Radio Theatre Collector's Edition; The Screwtape Letters by CS Lewis @2009 Tyndale House Publishers. (Snippets from Letter 3)

Consequently, Screwtape continues to advise on how to sweep Christians away with groupthink, popular self-centered notions that lead them farther away from understanding their unique giftings and purposes.

God knows you even better than you know yourself. He truly wants you to see yourself through His eyes. This is part of your journey in this series. As you meet Him and better understand the fullness of His Identity, you meet yourself and discover your Christ Identity, the ideal version of you that He sees you as already.

We can call on God by any of His Names that make Him real to us in the moment and learn directly from Him how to pray with authority the victories we need in life. Mike Noble from the Cleveland House of Prayer calls God the "trillion faceted diamond." He often asks people which facet(s) pierced their heart. Some have met the Provider and can trust Him with their provisional needs but don't know Him as their Friend. Others have met the Great Physician and trust God with their physical needs but not their emotional ones.

Our God is ALL those things and so much more. He wants you to allow more and more facets of the diamond to pierce your heart and transform you. He wants you to be free, whole, and victorious.

Galatians 5:25 says, "If we live by the Spirit, let us also walk by the Spirit."

It's Normal

God created everyone to see and hear Him with the eyes and ears of their heart. If you were unable to do so, you would never be able to close your eyes and picture a memory or hear in your mind a conversation you had or remember what you heard or saw in a film.

24

The screen of your mind gives you the ability to see, hear, and feel things. God created the eyes and ears of your heart, most importantly for you to connect with Him. In fact, without the eyes and ears of your heart, you never would have accepted Him as your Savior in the first place. God is not willing for any to perish, so He wired us to be able to communicate with Him.

> 2 Peter 3:9 (AMP) "The Lord does not delay [as though He were unable to act] and is not slow about His promise, as some count slowness, but is [extraordinarily] patient toward you, not wishing for any to perish but for all to come to repentance."

The entire Bible was written with the same four keys that you will use to encounter God. Two-thirds of the Bible was written through the "ears of the heart" as the human messengers wrote down what they heard straight from the Lord. The other third was written through the "eyes of the heart" as dreams and visions from the Lord were carefully recorded.

God was communicating messages from heaven. He is the same yesterday, today, and forever (Hebrews 13:8). So, if this is how God spoke to people in the days of the writing of the Bible, He surely can do it now! And even more so now that Christians have the indwelling Holy Spirit whose job it is to fill us with the power to connect with God's Nature and release His Love to others. This direct access to Father God is what Jesus accomplished for us on the cross.

Why the Special Place

In your first encounter that you will have in the next chapter, you will be taken to the **Special Place.** This is for you and Jesus privately. For some, it may be a beautiful location that brings them fond memories of the past. For others, it is a lovely place that they have never seen before. Jesus knows where your special place is, so do not try to figure that out or tell Him where it is. Just let yourself go wherever the Lord takes you.

The special place is essential because once you have seen Jesus there once, you can easily imagine going there again. You can expect to see Him there whenever you need.

He is not limited by this location. When you meet Him there, He can take you anywhere! Some of our encounters will not begin at the special place for specific reasons that will make sense. But I want you to get familiar with having a spiritual home base. Look around, see more of it as you go back for more experiences. The more you look, the more it will expand.

When I first saw my special place, it was no more than a back porch and a small grassy knoll. It has grown to include a flower path to the sea, a picturesque river and waterfall, a gazebo, a swing set, a dancefloor, and a unique tree. After two years and many adventures with Jesus in my special place, I got to see this place in the natural world in Israel. It was a short walk to the Sea of Galilee! It was incredible. I believe that many places on Earth are shadows of real majestic places in heaven. It was astonishing when I saw the similarities of my photos of that place to the descriptions I had written about it years before!

Jesus can take you anywhere once you begin. Not all your encounters on this journey will start in your special place. However, the more comfortable you are going there, the quicker you can meet Him, even if you are amid chaos or a crisis.

Film Clips, Lyric Videos and Collages

The Lord is creative. He wants to use as many aspects of the language of the heart to connect with you as possible. God has used media to communicate in each book that He has written through me. This time, the Lord wanted beautiful collages of our chapter lyric videos as a way for you to meditate on the words and connect even more with the songs. Additionally, there are some film clips to reinforce messages and guided imagery audio exercises that help to facilitate your encounters. As beautiful that they are in the book, you really must see them in color! Here is a link to all of them in color in addition to all media links in this book.

It is amazing to me how much more can be said in a song verse than can be said in pages of a book. The Lord wants you to exercise the eyes and ears of your heart in a variety of ways to strengthen them. Like physical muscles, the more you use them, the stronger they get.

All media links are found on the Experience Jesus page of PattySadallah.com and are identified by type of media and book page number. Keep this webpage open so you can simply click to the next media link in the book to watch, listen and experience everything without missing a beat!

Website: www.PattySadallah.com/Experience-Jesus.

God's Heart for You

The capacity to believe in Me is enlarged tremendously by experiencing Me! You encounter the Truth of who I AM to you personally, today, yesterday, and tomorrow when you fix your eyes on Me in all areas. I am sufficient for all of your needs. (see 2 Corinthians 12:9)

When you encounter Me by My Names personally, you begin to collect memories of Me being Who you need for each circumstance. This is how you will live your gospel story in the world and represent Me confidently. The more you encounter Me in these daily, personal ways, the more you give Me access to your heart for transformation.

Every name I have been for others in the Bible, I can be for you. Won't you allow Me to be them for you?

The Gospel is nothing more than a personal recounting of what you have seen, heard and experienced of God directly. When you encounter Me personally, you are a witness of the REAL God. Memories you collect with Me will increase your trust, faith, belief, and boldness to represent Me well in the world. The more you encounter the different aspects of Me, the more confidence you will have that I AM who I say I AM. The more confidence you have, the more you will inspire others to trust Me. Make them want what you have in Me.

Tell your story. Your story is your living gospel, your record of what I have done in your life. Share every character and aspect of Me you have ever met. Introduce people to Me as the Provider, Healer, Shepherd, Defender, Savior, Counselor, Friend, and Way Maker, Creator, etc. so they can know Me likewise.

*I am ready and waiting to meet you in these encounters. I am one God with many facets, way too large for anyone to understand completely. So, meet Me one Name at a time and build memories of personal times where you and I work through challenges and experience joy together. The more you encounter Me, the easier it will be to Trust Me and believe in Me in all areas of life. I Am the **Promise Keeper**. You'll see!*

The Names Addressed in Each Book

Book 1: How to Encounter the *LOVE* of God

1. When you meet the **Heavenly Father,** you are introduced to the power of child-like faith and its mysterious ability to help you connect with God purely and without the barriers to faith that adulthood brings.

2. When you meet the **Savior,** you learn in a most personal way, why the Lord chose to come as a human and died for YOU. You will understand the price paid for your salvation and why you were worth the cost to God. You will also appreciate the great exchange and the benefits that are yours now and forever as your inheritance.

3. When you meet **Immanuel,** you will encounter the God who always was, is, and always will be with you. He will show you that in an instant, you can see and feel His Covering and connect with His Mind, Will, and Emotion to handle any circumstance your days can bring.

4. When you meet the **Bridegroom,** you will understand the intimacy and value of God's genuine trust and partnership in your life. You will learn the benefits of being united to the All-powerful, All-knowing, All-benevolent, and Ever-Present God.

5. When you meet the **Friend,** you will encounter the joy of God as you have playful adventures with the One you trust with your heart, secrets, and life. You will learn about the powerful favor anointing that comes with the likeability factor of friendship and the role that praise and worship have in it.

Book 2: How to Encounter the *HEALING* of God

1. When you meet the **Great Physician,** He will show you the pathway to vibrant and abundant life. You will learn

how to tune to Him for clarity on all conditions that need to be met for physical healing and the relationship to spiritual, emotional, and mental health.

2. When you meet the **Comforter,** you will find the way to the peace that surpasses understanding by addressing past heart wounds and allowing Him to help you find forgiveness and give you a new heart.

3. When you meet the **Mighty Counselor,** you will learn how to spot the lies that keep you in bondage and trust God for the Truth that will set you free. Wisdom and understanding is found when you learn how to see your circumstances through God's eyes, ears, mind and heart.

4. When you meet the **Deliverer,** He will show you the way to find freedom from bondages by standing on His authority and exercising the authority you have by His power to live according to His promises.

5. When you meet the **Miracle Worker,** He will show you key principles for determining His will and accessing His power to pull miracles down from heaven according to His promises.

Book 3: How to Encounter the *DIRECTION* of God

1. When you meet the **Truth,** He will guide you to clarity, wisdom and understanding by interpreting scripture promises as they relate to your personal calling.

2. When you meet the **Shepherd,** you will see His gentle care, guidance, and protection as you learn to surrender your will and ways to His more perfect plan for you.

3. When you meet the **Author of your Story,** He will show you how to stay aligned to the ideal life plan that He has for you one day at a time.

4. When you meet the **Way Maker,** He will show you how He is working on your behalf often behind the scenes and without your awareness to equip you to accomplish your Kingdom purposes.

5. When you meet the **Supernatural Provider,** He will show to look beyond natural limitations for accomplishing your work for God. You will encounter His limitlessness and exercise your authority to receive supernatural provision for your Kingdom purposes.

Book 4: How to Encounter the *POWER* of God

1. When you meet the **Creator,** you will encounter the complexity and wonder of God and learn about the power of His spoken Word to create. Likewise, how you are made in His image to create as well.

2. When you meet **Almighty God,** you will encounter the Sovereign King of kings and get a greater sense of His Omni-Truths up close and personally. Limiting notions of God will be cast away.

3. When you meet **Defender,** God will show up as the one who fights on your behalf either on the spiritual warfare battlefield or in the Courts of Heaven. You will learn how and why you can access the defense of God in your everyday life.

4. When you meet the **Grace of God,** you will learn how to tap into the internal power of the Holy Spirit to live your most effective life without fears or limitations.

5. When you meet **Lord of Hosts,** He will show you the angelic realm as it's leader and teach you how to cooperate with the ministries of the angels assigned to protect and aid you throughout your life.

The Same Love by Paul Baloche

https://bit.ly/3gR8vtx

How to Encounter God

⟨⟨⟨⟩⟩⟩

*T*he conversations and adventures that you will have in this book are real spiritual encounters. They are not figments of your imagination. Believing this is the first step to having meaningful experiences with God.

By way of preparation for this journey, get yourself a journal. It can be as simple as a spiral bound notebook, or as I love to use, one that has Scripture verses at the bottom of every page. I have noticed when I use this kind of journal, that often exactly what Jesus or I am saying on the journal page is reinforced by the Scripture on that page. God is so cool like that!

This is your personal journey. God will call you by name. In fact, He may even give you a new pet name that no one else has ever called you. Stick with this, and I pray that Jesus will meet you one Name at a time exactly where you need Him. I don't know anyone who has encountered the **realness** of Jesus that has not been changed.

If you have not accepted Jesus as your LORD and Savior, this is an important step for you to work through. Appendix B has a special salvation prayer where you can dedicate or re-dedicate your life to

Jesus. We will cover this issue extensively when you meet the Savior in Book 1: Encountering the LOVE of God and He will seal this heart decision for all eternity so you can be assured of your salvation.

Finding God's Channel

The language of the heart is pictures, stories, music, emotions, and metaphors. Jesus demonstrated this by teaching through parables and stories relevant to the culture to connect with the hearts of the people at the time. The language of our heads is analytical and logical. Jesus reflected the character of His Father perfectly using the language of the heart. He spoke in the vernacular of their culture using common images of their day. He does the same thing today as you will see from the experiences that you, and all those for whom God has revealed Himself in this book series. You will learn how to tap into God's channel by putting your brain into the alpha state.

Alpha Brain Waves

Brain waves are measured by frequency, which is cycles per second, or hertz (Hz). They range from very slow to very fast. Alpha waves (8-12 Hz) fit in the middle of the spectrum, between beta and theta waves. Alpha is a state of alert relaxation and fosters creativity. Children from the age of 2 to 8 live primarily in the alpha brain state. They are too young to worry and simply go with the flow of life with play and creative imagination. [4]

Your brain produces the alpha waves when you are not concentrating on anything in particular. For example, when you are driving and realize that your mind has been wandering, but you are still able to keep your eyes on the road, you are in alpha.

---

4 https://blog.mindvalley.com/science-behind-brainwaves/

In the Heavenly Father chapter of Book 1, you realize the importance of approaching God as a child as it naturally connects you with the alpha state and brings the faith of a child. We meet this Name of God first because it is crucial always to meet Him as a child. It took me about two years to realize how important this is to connect with God more effectively.

The alpha brain wave is one of the factors that help you tune into God's channel. You can easily learn the skill of putting your brain in alpha. In fact, the Dialogue Journaling tool we use to encounter God does just that! When your brain is producing these waves as part of your encountering experiences with Jesus, the results can reduce your stress levels and help you feel calmer, more loved, and most importantly, closer to a personal God.

Theta is the brain wave of logical thinking. Most adults spend their waking hours in theta. The brain wave looks more like an active lie detector with fast ups and downs, whereas the alpha state appears as slower rolling hills.

Biblical Meditation

The Bible includes 20 verses to encourage us to meditate on the Word.

> Psalm 104: 34 *May my meditation be pleasing to Him, as I rejoice in the LORD.*

Meditation is a heart posture whereby you surrender all the faculties of your brain to the Lord to gain His wisdom and insight. Wait, doesn't this seem like the stuff that the new agers do? Isn't meditation their word? Sure, but it was God's word first. Do you know why no one counterfeits a three-dollar bill? It is because there is no real $3.00 bill, and it's not a valuable number. The enemy is a counterfeiter. If the new agers are doing it, then something about it is a bit off and was swindled from what is real and valuable.

Let's look at the differences: New Agers seek to connect with the spirit realm when they meditate. They also relax to put their brains into an alpha state. But they seek to connect with spirits in general. We aim to connect with Jesus. This is an important distinction.

> Matthew 7:9-11 (AMP) [9] Or what man is there among you who, if his son asks for bread, will [instead] give him a stone? [10] Or if he asks for a fish, will [instead] give him a snake? [11] If you then, evil (sinful by nature) as you are, know how to give good and advantageous gifts to your children, how much more will your Father who is in heaven [perfect as He is] give what is good and advantageous to those who keep on asking Him.

The Word promises that if you ask for Jesus, you get Jesus. If you ask for generalized spirits, the enemy will surely oblige. Never seek to speak or pray to dead family members or anyone other than God when meditating. The Strong's Exhaustive Concordance defines meditation: "to murmur; to converse with oneself, and hence aloud; speak; talk; babbling; communication; mutter; roar; mourn; a murmuring sound; a musical notation; to study; to ponder; revolve in your mind; imagine; pray; prayer; reflection; devotion.[5] It is a surrender of your entire mind to God's Spirit to meditate on Him. The left-brained activities include reason, written language, and speech. The right-brained activities are related to music, art awareness, intuition, and imagination.

You have all these characteristics included if you look at the meditation definition through the filter of all the left- and right activities of the brain.

5 https://Biblehub.com/hebrew/yehgeh_1897.htm search word Strongs Concordance for "meditation"

Dialogue Journaling

We will be using dialogue journaling as our primary tool for connecting with God. Dr. Mark Virkler came up with four simple keys to hearing God's voice[6] from more than 11 years an unrelenting heart desire to commune with God personally. This simple statement summarizes the four keys: Hearing from God is as simple as 1) quieting yourself down, 2) fixing your eyes on Jesus, 3) tuning to spontaneity, and 4) writing it down. These are the steps for what Virkler calls the skill of dialogue journaling or two-way journaing.

1. **Quiet yourself down**- externally and internally

2. **Fix your Eyes on Jesus**- ask and expect to see, hear, and feel from Him

3. **Tune to spontaneity**- allow the pictures, thoughts, and feelings to bubble up without self-effort.

4. **Write down** what you saw, heard, felt and thought.

The entire Bible was written by God speaking or showing someone something spontaneously and them writing it down so others could read it. Habakkuk 2:1-2 demonstrates these steps beautifully. Habakkuk was a prophet at the time when the Lord was exiling the Jews to other nations for what would be 70 years. The prophet was perplexed by why the Israelites were being taken away and wanted to talk to God about it. The four key steps are revealed in Habakkuk 2:1-2:

Verse segment/ How it relates to the Four Keys

> [1] *I will stand on my guard post and station myself on the rampart;* / Habakkuk found a quiet place so he could look up to God. He was posturing his heart to speak to God Himself.

---

6 *4 Keys to Hearing God's Voice* by Drs Mark and Patti Virkler, CWG Ministries

And I will keep watch to see what He will speak to me,/ He was looking and listening with an expectation to hear from God personally, using the eyes and ears of his heart.

And how I may reply when I am reproved./ Habakkuk knew it would be a conversation with God. He knew that he could hear what God had to say, AND that he could reply to God.

²Then the LORD answered me and said,/ God did reply personally.

"Record the vision and inscribe it on tablets, so the one who reads it may run."/ God commanded Habakkuk to write down what He was saying. Writing it down is not just for you to remember, but it can also become a blessing for others.

Managing Expectations

Your first exercise will help you with all future exercises. God will take you to your *special place* where you and He will have your first encounter. Your conversations and adventures can begin in this place and Jesus can take you anywhere He wants from there. Getting familiar with your spiritual place will help you comfortably anchor your memories with Jesus. The more you go there, the more He will expand it so you can see and experience more there.

Before we begin, I wanted to manage some expectations. God's voice does not sound like an external, booming or roaring voice. As we have already learned, it sounds like your own thoughts, pictures, emotions, and songs but is spontaneous with God's character and nature. So, don't jam the receiver with unrealistic expectations that an James Earl Jones-esque voice needs to be speaking in an audible voice for it to be God.

Let's practice using the eyes and ears of the heart right now. Wherever you are, close your eyes. If you are in your bedroom, picture your kitchen or another room in your house. "Look" on the screen of your mind and scan the room. Notice the details that you see. They may not be as clear as if your eyes were open looking at that room, but I'm willing to bet that you have clear impressions in your mind of those rooms. You were just using the eyes of your heart.

Now, close your eyes and begin to sing the Happy Birthday song in your mind. Hear it? That's you using the ears of your heart. If you could hear and see in those quick examples, then you can be sure that you can hear and see Jesus when you ask for Him.

We know that He will show up when you do because He wants to connect with you even more than you want to communicate with Him. God answers yes to heart desires that are in alignment with His will. This means that when you agree to meet with God, He shows up and moves to align you according to His will.

If at first you don't see him in 3D vivid color, that's perfectly OK. You can be grateful with glimpses, sounds, smells, pictures, feelings or single words initially. Don't allow your expectations to rob you of blessings by dismissing the small beginnings. It will get easier with practice. The more you dialogue journal, the more you will be able to see and hear God.

Hopefully, by the end of this book experience, you and Jesus will be intimate friends and you will be seeing and hearing from Him like a pro. Give yourself some learning curve time. Practice makes perfect. You will meet Jesus in your special place and then He will take the scene where it needs to go.

Encounter Jesus: Your Special Place

Have your notebook or journal handy to record your experience. For many of the encounters in this book series, there will be guided imagery links where you can listen to my voice as a guide. Not every encounter will need this as you get more experienced with your special place. All guided imageries and lyric video links can be found on my website www.PattySadallah.com/Experience-Jesus Keep this page open as you read through the book so those links are handy. They are easily identified by book page number and title.

Special Place Encounter

You can experience this first *special place* encounter by clicking this link http://bit.ly/2g8v8iu. Just relax and listen as I walk you through your first Jesus encounter. Make sure you record what you see and hear Jesus doing with you.

If you do not have a computer, find someone who will talk through these steps for you. It would be too difficult to keep your eyes on Jesus and keep track of these steps as you go. Make sure you keep the experience going long past when the audio instruction has finished. Don't jam the receiver on God just because the audio instruction is complete.

Here are the steps to this encountering experience of meeting Jesus in your special place: Get in a comfortable position where you will not be disturbed. Relax.

- For best results, spend time worshipping and praising Him even before you open in prayer to welcome His presence.

- Begin with a prayer that welcomes God and invites Him to come speak to you today. You are only wanting to speak to

Jesus. Let Him know that He is who you desire to meet with today.

- Let God show you a beautiful place. It could be somewhere you have been before that brings you comfort, or it could be a paradise-like place from your imagination. He knows the place, so just relax.

- With the eyes of your heart, take your time to look carefully on the screen of your mind to the left, to the right, directly in front of you, up above your head, and then down.

- Take in all that you can see, hear, and smell of this place. Awaken all your senses. But don't judge or try harder regarding how much you can see at first.

- After getting a picture in your mind of this place, turn around and see Jesus walking toward you. Don't strain with the eyes of your heart, just relax and allow yourself to see and sense what you can.

- See Jesus come all the way up to you and give you a big loving hug. Feel His embrace. Soak in the feeling of His Presence.

- Sit, lay down or begin walking with Jesus. Ask Him a question. These questions will change as you work through this book. Your first question is: How do you feel about me LORD? Tune to flowing pictures, thoughts and emotions, as these are coming from the Spirit within (Jn. 7:37-39).

- Allow Jesus to completely take over the scene. Watch, listen, and feel what He is doing.

- Write down what you see Him doing, saying, and showing you. Don't question it, just write it down in simple child-like faith.

- Feel free to ask Him another question. Keep the conversation going like you would with a dear friend. The more you do, the more He will show you.

- Let Jesus keep speaking and showing you what He wants until you feel like the conversation has ended.

Give thanks for whatever you got from Jesus. It may be that you could only get a feeling, or a small picture, or one word. Anything you receive is a good start.

If you haven't been recording the experience as it is happening, write it down now. Thank God for what He showed you. Consult Appendix A for more tips on Hearing God's voice. You will get more skilled at this as you work through the book.

Each time you encounter God, ask for Him to give you more. If you are seeing pictures, ask Him to explain what they mean. If you hear Him clearly, ask Him for more visions. Remember to thank Him no matter what He gives you!

How He Loves Us By David Crowder Band

https://bit.ly/2PNFe7a

Encountering the LOVE of God
Introduction

Everything that God does is motivated by love. Love is not a thing He feels, it is who He is! The entire Bible is one elaborate love story. In this book, you will meet the tender side of God's nature and character. When taking the Biblical Research Methods class for my doctorate, I was to research a topic extensively using a variety of biblical research tools. Initially, when I began seeking the Lord for this project's theme, the Lord gave me just the word; "love." Love is such a big word. This topic category was overwhelming for me.

I consulted the Lord through journaling, and this is what He said:

> *Pattycake,*
> *I want you to know the meaning of the love I wrote to you about in the letter I gave you when you were saved. Look at it again. Follow the trail that it takes you. I speak in it of an everlasting love. Look at this letter and the key aspects of love that are in it. They are the ones I want you to explore. Make this a personal journey. When you learn more about My love, you will be more able to love. I AM God believe it and be satisfied!*

Your journey begins as it did for you in 1979 – with that first love letter. It will show you the way!

It's astonishing to me how many times the Lord has spoken to me through this love letter! In my first book, *Clips That Move Mountains*, I wrote about the miraculous story of receiving this letter from God on the heels of my salvation in 1979 directly after being led to Christ by an angel. In that book, I share how the letter was lost to me for decades before God gave it back to me so I could share it in that book.

Here it was again, the central resource for my biblical research project on love. That journey would turn into an intertwining understanding of what love has to do with our callings. The *Encountering the DIRECTION of God Book 3* of this book series will dive into that topic more in-depth..

God's Original Love Letter to Me

But for now, the emphasis is love. Here is that original message from the Lord:

> *Everyone longs to give themselves completely to someone – to have a deep soul relationship with another, to be loved thoroughly and exclusively. But God, to a Christian says:*
>
> *"No, not until you are satisfied and fulfilled and content with being loved by Me alone. I love you, my child, and until you discover that only in Me is your satisfaction to be found, you will not be capable of the perfect human relationship that I have planned for you. You'll never be united with another until you are united with Me – exclusive of anyone or anything else, exclusive of any other desires or longings. I want you to stop planning, stop wishing, and allow Me to give you the most thrilling plan existing – one that you can't imagine. I*

want you to have the best. Please allow Me to bring it to you. Just keep experiencing that satisfaction of knowing that I AM. Keep learning and listening to the things I tell you... You must wait.

Don't be anxious. Don't worry. Don't look around at the things others have gotten or that I've given to them. Don't look at the things you think you want. You just keep looking off and away up to Me, or you'll miss what I want to show you.

Then, when you're ready, I'll surprise you with the love far more wonderful than any would ever dream. You see, until you are ready and until the one I have for you is ready, I'm working even this very minute to have both of you ready at the same time. Until you are both satisfied exclusively with Me and with the life I have prepared for you, you won't be able to experience the love that exemplifies your relationship with Me... And this is the perfect love.

And dear one, I want you to have this most wonderful love, I want you to see in flesh a picture of your relationship with Me, and enjoy materially and concretely the everlasting union of beauty and perfection and love that I offer you with Myself.

Know that I love you utterly, I AM God. Believe it and be satisfied."

When I received this love letter in 1979, I had only been a believer for a couple of days. When I read it, I felt comfort believing that it was a promise from the Lord that He would bring me a future husband. At that time in my spiritual development, it was a letter about helping a heart-broken girl in this world.

When the Lord gave that letter back to me in 2012 when I was writing *Clips that Move Mountains*, I could see that the "true love" was not a human, but God Himself. I saw it as a message about the need for an intimate relationship with Him. I still didn't see the connection between His love and my calling.

After this Biblical research assignment, I was able to see more layers of meaning in that love letter. Now I can see that being satisfied, fulfilled, and content in this life is related to the closeness of my relationship with God. The more I encounter the Lord personally, the more I can see, feel, and think like Him. The more His love is **real** to me, the more I can walk in His love and trust Him with everything. The letter shows me that God is ALL and is in ALL.

You cannot love anyone properly or at all, aside from God, least of all yourself. Love comes from God and flows to you and then out to others. If you want a perfect human relationship, it will come only with the surrender, humility, and faith that comes from conforming your heart to God's. This is His transformational way.

God had me share this letter with you because even though He gave it to me, it's for you too! God created all of us to desire to be loved thoroughly and exclusively. Apart from God, it is impossible to be loved the way He created you to need love. You must find your way to the Author of love. God wants to be your one true love, *exclusive of anything or anyone else*. He is saying that He wants you to lay down all the idols in your heart and fix your eyes on Jesus alone. The more you are with Him, the more you will become like Him, and the more useful you will be to the Kingdom.

He shared with me that satisfaction comes from knowing that *"I AM."* This kind of knowing is of the most personal type. He wants you to have the satisfaction of His very presence in your life too. You trust people that you know, like and have found to be honest and trustworthy.

This trust can only grow with time and intimacy together. Your faith comes from trusting Him alone the same way that you do for other people. The only difference is His perfection. His love will never let you down!

He is preparing you to keep watching, looking, and keeping your eyes on HIM always, so you don't miss what He has for you and go off on bunny trails of distraction. When you begin to have experiences with God's love by these Name encounters in your spiritual special place, your heart and soul will begin to anchor soundly in God's love. The more experiences you have with Him, the more your heart and soul will trust Him, and you will change. You will begin to reflect the Fruit of the Spirit.

> Galatians 5:22-23 22 But the fruit of the Spirit [the result of His Presence within us] is love [unselfish concern for others], joy, [inner] peace, patience [not the ability to wait, but how we act while waiting], kindness, goodness, faithfulness, 23 gentleness, self-control. Against such things there is no law.

Stay the course! It's is all about becoming who God sees you as already. The Lord showed me -

> 2 Corinthians 3:18 18 And we all, with unveiled face, continually seeing as in a mirror the glory of the Lord, are progressively being transformed into His image from [one degree of] glory to [even more] glory, which comes from the Lord, [who is] the Spirit.

> *It is My will that all of My believers may grasp this truth; that you would see in the mirror the unveiled face that is stripped away of the pride of 'you,' that is, the best version of yourself 'you.' It's your Christ Identity or Christ-I for short. Because you continue to behold Me, keeping your eyes locked, fixed,*

unmoving off Me, you will begin to see Me when you look in the mirror. The glory of the Lord is My character, and that's the transformation I see in you. That's the calling I have for you and for the ones I have for you to influence.

Why these Names?

The five Names of God that you will meet in the pages of this book and in your spirit are intimate and show you the tender sides of God. These are aspects of God's character and roles He plays that make you feel safe, loved, and help you to see who you are to God; how He truly sees you. These Christ-I truths are foundational to receiving His healing, direction, and power, addressed by meeting the names covered in the other three books of this series. So, we begin with meeting Love Himself.

When you meet the **Heavenly Father,** you are introduced to the power of child-like faith and its mysterious ability to help you connect with God purely and without the barriers to faith that adulthood brings.

When you meet the **Savior**, you learn in a most personal way, why the Lord chose to come as a human and die for YOU. You will better understand the price paid for your salvation and why you were worth the cost to God and the great exchange you received when you accepted Him.

When you meet **Immanuel,** you will encounter the God who always was, is, and always will be with you. He will show you that in an instant, you can see and feel His covering and connect with His mind, will, and emotion to handle any circumstance your days can bring.

When you meet the **Bridegroom,** you will understand the intimacy and value of God's true partnership in your life. You will learn the benefits of being united to the All-powerful, All-knowing, All-Benevolent, and Ever-Present God.

When you meet the **Friend,** you will encounter the joy of God as you have playful adventures with the One you trust with your heart, secrets, and life. You will learn about the powerful favor anointing that comes when you become God's friend.

I Wanna Go Back by David Dunn

https://bit.ly/2DFkxbc

Meet the Heavenly Father

❧

*I*f you are like me, your father association is not idyllic. I think it's safe to say that many would say their relationship with their natural father or father figures does not inspire thoughts of unconditional love. Unfortunately, many of us struggle with connecting to the Heavenly Father because our fathers were not people for whom we felt particularly safe or loved. This negative association makes connecting with the Heavenly Father a bit of a challenge for some. But this is the reason it is crucial to meet this aspect of God personally.

Jesus made constant note of communicating His identity associated with His Father. His very destiny on earth related to His role as God's Son: to bring us to the Father and to show us *how* to connect with Him.

> John 14:6 (AMP) ⁶ Jesus *said to him, "I am the way, and the truth, and the life; no one comes to the Father but through Me."

Later in that chapter, the disciples ask Jesus to tell them more about the Heavenly Father, and He replies:

John 14: 7 (AMP) If you had known Me, you would have known My Father also; from now on you know Him and have seen Him."

Jesus' connection with His Holy Father was critical to His life and role on earth as our Savior and Redeemer. He and the Father are ONE. They are united, intertwined. Jesus and His Father share the same characteristics.

Is-ness and Omni-truths

In my Just Ask Jesus book *How to Live a Worry-Free Life*, we looked at the "Is-ness" of God. That is the Omni-Truths about God that were, are, and always will be who He is. These were the truths about God that existed long before He created the heavens, earth, or you.

- **Omni-benevolence-** God is love and all that it reflects. Galatians 5:22-23 [22] But the fruit of the Spirit [the result of His Presence within us] is love [unselfish concern for others], joy, [inner] peace, patience [not the ability to wait, but how we act while waiting], kindness, goodness, faithfulness, [23] gentleness, self-control. Against such things there is no law.

- **Omniscience-** God knows all and is the source of all knowledge and wisdom. Psalm 147:5 Great is our [majestic and mighty] Lord and abundant in strength; His understanding is inexhaustible [infinite, boundless].

- **Omnipresence-** God is self-existing and is everywhere present - yesterday, today, and tomorrow and sees all. He never leaves or for forsakes us. Job 34:21 "For God's eyes are on the ways of a man, And He sees all his steps.

- **Omnipotence**- God is all-powerful. Almighty God, all strength comes from Him. In 1 Chronicles 29:11, It says "Yours, O LORD, is the greatness and the power and the glory and the victory and the majesty, indeed everything that is in the heavens and on the earth; Yours is the dominion *and* kingdom, O LORD, and You exalt Yourself as head over all."

The Heavenly Father explains this for us in this next journal conversation.

Super Dad

Lord, please help us understand Your name, Heavenly Father.

When you think of Me as your Father, I don't want you to filter Me through the lens of your natural father. Even if your earthly father did the best job he could, looking at Me this way will severely limit your understanding of the truth of Me as Heavenly Father. No one is perfect apart from Me.

It's better if you picture Me as Super Dad.

Reflect for a moment on My Omni-Truths. Imagine Me as a Father that is perfectly fair in all circumstances, who unconditionally loves you; who sees and has been with you every single moment of your life. I live outside of time and space, so I have already seen how your life turns out. You can trust Me to guide you. I'm a perfectly wise Dad.

There is no area of your life that I can't guide you. After all, I AM the Truth and hold all knowledge and wisdom in the palms of My hands. I will protect you and fight your battles for you because I AM your strength. I am the Father that builds you up, and that guides you along the paths to your perfect destiny with Me (Jeremiah 29:11). As your Safe Father, I can never break a promise. There is no fear in coming near Me, only unconditional love. I'm Super Dad!

You can encounter Me as Super Dad, even if you have/had an unloving father. I can heal those negative associations and give you a far more satisfying adult childhood. It's time to be a kid again! Just let Me show you how!

Bedknobs and Broomsticks Dream:

Before I had the dream I will share below; I had been praying with this lady for many hours for relief of chronic pain and deliverance. The Lord communicated clearly that the condition of her healing was that she needed to forget everything she thought she knew about Him, come as a child, and simply believe Him for her healing.

Even though this message was for her, it stuck with me. That condition for her healing was the moment that God highlighted the importance of childlike faith and the Name Heavenly Father for me. I began earnest research on the subject and switched my special place encounters from that day on to encountering Jesus only as a child.

It was after a day of reflection on this issue that I had a dream. Just like in the movie; *Bedknobs & Broomsticks* from the 1960's, I was at the foot of a large bed. There were other people at the front of the bed trying to make it fly. They were twisting the bed knobs, and we flew up in the air and then immediately dropped back to the ground. It was a jarring experience. I was holding on to the edges of the bed, shouting, "You are making this too difficult! It is so much easier than you think!" I was frustrated! Then I woke up.

Lord, please help me understand this dream.

You've been trying to help many people that are struggling with their faith. Their unbelief is a barrier to their healing. Miracles seem illogical to them, like being able to fly in a bed. But childlike faith is essential to living the victorious Christian life.

Why Childlike Faith is Essential

Essential. Hmmm. That's a powerful word. I thought I had better find out why.

Mark 10:13-16 (AMP) [13] People were bringing children to Him so that He would touch *and* bless them, but the disciples reprimanded them *and* discouraged them [from coming]. [14] But when Jesus saw this, He was indignant, and He said to them, "Allow the children to come to Me; do not forbid them; for the kingdom of God belongs to such as these. [15] I assure you *and* most solemnly say to you, **whoever does not receive *and* welcome the kingdom of God like a child will not enter it at all.**" [16] And He took the children [one by one] in His arms and [a]blessed them [with kind, encouraging words], placing His hands on them.

Remember the story of Peter Pan, when he went into the bedroom of the children and taught them about flying? He told them that if they had pixie dust sprinkled on them and thought about happy thoughts (that they spoke out loud by the way), and took the leap, they would fly. So, Peter sprinkled fairy dust on them, and they spoke happy words.

PUPPIES, ICE CREAM AND CHRISTMAS!!! And then they jumped and were able to fly.

Yes, I do remember that, Lord. My daughter used to watch that movie over and over when she was a kid.

Fairy dust is like the magical power of childlike faith. The happy thoughts are the Biblical truths that need to be declared out loud because they agree with God's Truth. The leaping is like stepping out in faith as if what they are praying for is already true and real. Remember that faith is not seeing then believing, it's believing before you see because it IS already true in My heavenly realm. Active faith makes it manifest in the natural world.

Childlike Faith + Speaking Biblical Truth + Faithful Action = Victory/ Freedom/Healing

All three of those steps are necessary for victory. Miss a part of that formula, and the equation doesn't work. An insincere heart speaking Truth without faith or action will only benefit so much.

A lack of cooperation also reveals a lack of faith. For some to come to Me with childlike faith is a significant challenge. They have had so much untrue and limiting programming in their lives, it's hard to separate the Truth for them.

What needs to happen is a heart reset, like a computer that needs to be reset to a time before the problems, viruses, and issues began wrecking it. Some stuff is lost when there is a computer reset, but you can have a clean slate. It's like getting a brand-new computer.

Go back to the time when you were not yet spoiled by a religious spirit, wounded by rejection, the pain of life circumstances, judgments, or loss of innocence. Picture yourself and find a photo of yourself between the ages of four and eight. Meditate on the photo and on your memories of an incredibly happy time (happy thoughts). Remember what it was like to be that age. I know, for many, there was pain even at this age. Ask Me to show you a memory when you were happy and innocent. I was there! You have more happy memories than you think! I remember them all!

Then while still relating to your younger self, meet Me in the special place and let Me take you on a sweet adventure that will remind you of who you were and still truly are to Me. Meeting Me as a child will help you get over unbelief and give you the faith you need to work through the rest of the formula that leads to victory, freedom, and healing.

5-year old me on my birthday

Why Children Believe

The first key to hearing God's voice is to quiet yourself down. The reason this is important is that it begins to dial your brain down to an alpha brainwave. Alpha is the brainwave of imagination, REM dream sleep, and overall relaxation. It is natural for children to use their imagination, believe, see pictures, stories, and have playfulness at their core. There is a trusting, believing innocence in children that is only unlearned as they grow or encounter rejection and pain.

I was privileged to be an advisor for Dr. Isabelle Knockeart Declerq's dissertation entitled *The Power of Childlike Faith* for her Christian Leadership University Doctorate.[7] In her thesis, she asserts: "Children between 0-8 don't "interpret" or process the world around them. It's the world they live in that matters. They believe what they experience with the senses of their hearts because they function like that. They are brain-wired to function this way. Trying to correct them and force our rationalized worldview upon them constantly is like intruding even abusing their inner being"... "God lives in our past and our present and in our future. He is omnipresent in every dimension; the permanent, eternal, consistent Father God. Children get that reality because they haven't been trapped rationally in a timeframe yet. They still live in absolutes: total trust, total feeling, completely happy or completely sad, playful or sleeping, laughing or crying"... "Their faith capacities are still intact, and their inner senses very pure and vivid."

Another factor that affects us as we grow out of childhood is our culture that communicates and rewards logic and rationalism over emotions and imagination. Children, when they hit the educational system, quickly learn what is rewarded and what is not.

When we quiet ourselves down so that we may hear God's voice, we put our bodies in the God TV channel of alpha brainwave mode.

At first, what we're trying to do is quiet natural noises and distractions, external factors. But what we need to learn how to do

---

7 *The Power of Childlike Faith,* by Dr. Isabelle Knockaert Declerq Dissertation submitted for PhD of Christian Counseling, Christian Leadership University 2019

is turn inwardly and quiet our spirits. Imagining yourself as a small child causes you to turn inwardly and connect with your inner child at that age.

Walking on Water

It's fascinating that when you picture yourself as a five-year-old child in your spirit, you think, feel and behave like a five-year-old child in your Jesus encounter. Two years before learning this lesson, the Lord had me experience walking on water as Peter did in the Bible.

I had been meditating on the *Oceans* song by Hillsong United, and the Lord took me to that scene, and I experienced it. Below was my recounting of that first experience. Remember, in this encounter, I am picturing myself as an adult.

I was reading the story about when Jesus and Peter walked on water when the Oceans song began playing in the background. I asked the Lord to show me this scene personally.

I was on the boat. It was rocking back and forth violently. Water was pouring over the ship at each wave. I was terrified. Someone said they could see a figure, maybe a ghost. It was Jesus calmly walking toward the boat. The water was washing over him, but his stride was steady. He was not affected by this storm.

I imagined myself being Peter and wanting to walk out to Jesus. I started with so much courage. I jumped out of the boat and began walking on water. I had a rush of adrenaline and felt so good. I just kept looking at Jesus and taking one step at a time. Then a wave engulfed me, and I was terrified. I started to sink. I could suddenly feel the violence of the water, and I went far below the surface. Then

I felt Jesus grab my arm. He effortlessly lifted me into His arms and kept walking toward the boat. He gently tossed me onto the boat and then told the storm to calm down, and the waters were still. Jesus turned and said:

> *"You did just fine while your eyes were fixed on Me. Keep your eyes fixed on Me, and you will always be safe. No storm can overtake you when your eyes are fixed on Me."*

That was a fantastic lesson to learn. A couple of years later, while I was in the midst of the childlike faith research, I heard the *Oceans* song on the radio, and it took me back to my encounter. Then the Lord spoke in my Spirit:

> *Pattycake, I want you to have that 'walk on water' experience again, only now, come to Me as a child.*

I was jumping like a kid in a puddle. Jesus and I were splashing and giggling. It was great fun! Then the big wave came over my head, and ... all I did was cling to Jesus. I just grabbed on and wouldn't let go. That's what kids do. They grab onto the one they trust will take care of them. Kids don't worry about the bills, or jobs, or taxes. When something scary happens, they cling to the person that makes them feel safe.

I know that many of you have had crummy childhoods. I know mine was not all peaches and cream. And some of you had to grow up way too fast and can't even remember a happy childhood moment. But Jesus was there, and He knows that there is an innocent, loving, trusting kid inside of you. He can help you find that child in you again. I have noticed something about my inner child for whom I encounter Jesus. She is more confident and happier than I remember being as a child. Because she is the real inner me. Not the one that was already being quenched by the world or by imperfect parenting. Allow your inner child to break forth and you will see major healing in your life. We address this more in Book 2: Encountering the Healing of God.

One lady I know confessed that she didn't have one single happy memory of childhood. And if you knew her story, you would not be surprised. But she prayed that Jesus would show her at least one loving, innocent and trusting memory for which to re-connect to her inner child. God gave her five!

Missions Trip to the Inner Child Dream

I dreamt that the ladies from our Spirit Life Circle were meeting at a camp. I saw my sister drive up as an adult, but when she opened the car door, she was a 5-year-old girl. We were all 5-year-old girls. I hugged her, and we turned around and saw that the welcome banner over the camp entrance said, "*Mission's Trip to the Inner Child.*"

Jesus was our Camp Counselor, and we had such an amazing day of fun with Him. We swam in the pool, rolled down the hill, finger painted, and drew pictures. We sang songs and laughed a lot with Jesus. He told us to get Him some flowers and then come back and bring them to Him as a gift. We were running all over the grass, picking up dandelions and making them into bouquets in our tiny hands. I remember that dandelion weeds were flowers to us when we were kids. One of the kids squealed with delight because she found the biggest patch of "roses!"

We stood in line, much like kids do waiting for their turn with Santa, and then climbed upon His lap to give Him our flower gifts. He talked with each of us like we were the only child there. He smiled and then whispered the Truth that would set us free in each of our ears.

When it was over, I reflected that I really did feel five years old again. I had the care-free thoughts, innocence and trust of a child. The Lord wanted these ladies to experience what I dreamed and told me to prepare the group for this encounter for our next meeting.

On the day of our circle time, I brought finger paints, colored pencils, scented markers, and crayons, drawing tablets and coloring books and playdough. The smells and activities took us back to our days in kindergarten. As we did our opening prayer and listened to our worship song, we played with these materials. Many remembered and re-created a specific picture they would draw in kindergarten like a house with a pathway and tree or horses and a barn.

When it was time to journal, I led them through the encounter of the same experiences I had in the dream culminating with sitting on Jesus' lap and having Him whisper the Truth that would set them free. Some people were taken back to memories that Jesus healed at that moment. Others received physical healings that day. It was miraculous!

I have since had many adventures with Jesus as a child. I always encounter Him as a child now. When we imagine ourselves as children, our trust and faith have no boundaries. We are much more open to receiving from God in this posture.

 Encountering the Heavenly Father

Remember Me Encounter – *https://bit.ly/2XYonDc*

If you have a hard time picturing a happy time as a child and struggle to connect with God as a loving Father, begin with this encounter.

- Go to your special place and meet Father God there. Share your heart with Him about your challenge to either seeing Him as a Father or becoming like a child. Ask Him to show you a memory of a happy time in your life. He was there, and He knows the one that you need to see.

- He will take you back to that time and place and allow you to see and feel that childlike joy. This time, you will see Jesus or Father God with you. He was there, so this is a real picture of your memory.

***The Mission's Trip to the Inner Child* Encounter** – *https:// bit.ly/30QWtuH*

If possible, find a photo of yourself between the ages of 4-8 years old. Specifically, one with the joy of childhood on your face. I have found the one that the Lord wants me to use, and it is attached. If a photo is not available, remember a specific time within that age window that made you especially happy and picture in your imagination that time of your life, or moment of joy, remembering it and holding it close to your heart. Looking at this photo will help you imagine and remember what it was like to be that young.

Steps of the Encounter

- Relax and welcome God's presence. Thank Him for what He is about to show you.

- See yourself as a child driving in the back of a car with your backpack

- The car stops, you get out and you see the Camp banner *Mission's Trip to the Inner Child*

- Jesus comes to greet you with a big smile. He is your camp counselor.

- He picks you up and swings you around. He is so happy you are there.

- Jesus tells you that you can do anything you want with Him in this camp and suggests a few choices. Swimming, horseback riding, drawing, or crafts, or playing at the beach.

- Spend a few minutes doing one or two of those things...

- The sun is starting to set so Jesus is building a campfire so you can have smores soon.

- He asks you to go get Him some flowers as a gift while He tends to the fire.

- Then He motions you back and you sit on His lap and give Him your flower gift.

- Then he whispers into your ear how much He loves you and tells you the Truth that will set you free.

- Take all the time you need here with Him and make sure you record this entire experience in your journal.

Love Letter to God- Meditate on your blessings and praise and worship for a bit. Write a love letter to the Heavenly Father. Go to your special place as a child and present your letter to Him. Then let Him show you how He feels about it!

Still Rolling Stones by Lauren Daigle

https://bit.ly/2XWHMUV

Meet the Savior

〰️

*D*o you remember the moment that the Lord Jesus Christ pierced your heart? Think back on the day of your salvation. Remember the emotion, surrender, hope and excitement of it. Or, perhaps that day is in the future for you. Maybe that day is today.

I remember a day I said no to Jesus. I attended a youth group retreat when I was about 15 years old. It was not from my Catholic Church but a non-denominational church. I don't remember why my sister and I were there or why my mother would let me go to a non-Catholic overnight event. It was certainly out of her character to do so.

I was more enamored with a boy there than what the youth leaders were preaching. But I heard enough to understand salvation for the first time. I remember saying no in my spirit. I think I was really saying, not now. I felt I was going to say yes someday. Yet, I didn't want to give up on fun things for which I assumed from my religious upbringing was the price of salvation. Suffering, poverty, performance, and earning God's love were reinforced messages in my upbringing. So, I said, no.

I remember being in third grade and my teacher, a nun at the Catholic school, asked the kids if they wanted to be a "saint" when they grew up. It was unanimous! NO ONE wanted to be a saint. The most memorable answer to the question was, "Because you have to be dead." The whole class laughed at that one! The truth is that every born-again Christian is a saint.

> Colossians 1:11-14 (AMP) [11] [we pray that you may be] strengthened and invigorated with all power, according to His glorious might, to attain every kind of endurance and patience with joy; [12] giving thanks to the Father, who has qualified us to share in the inheritance of the saints (God's people) in the Light.

> [13] For He has rescued us and has drawn us to Himself from the dominion of darkness, and has transferred us to the Kingdom of His beloved Son, [14] in whom we have redemption [because of His sacrifice, resulting in] the forgiveness of our sins [and the cancellation of sins' penalty].

I shared the story of my "yes" to salvation in my *Clips that Move Mountains* book. It is a wild story of how God used an angel to bring me to Him. Then immediately allowed for heartbreak, and God sent me the love letter. It was my first journal from the Lord, which came only two days after my salvation. The Lord used it to comfort me and put me on the path of seeking His face. I lost that letter for twenty-four years until God brought it back to me so I could share it in my books. God continues to use it to change my life and others in ever-peeling onion layers to this day.

Since then, I have experienced slow and steady growth, seasons of backsliding, and then, sky rocketing faith, once I learned how to connect with God's realness. These truths are what I write about in all my books and classes. It all begins with your "YES!"

Why Did Jesus Come and Die for Us?

God created the universe and everyone in it so that He could have direct communion with us. Everything God does is motivated by this Love. The Lord walked with Adam and Eve in the cool of the day and fellowshipped with them face to face. All was well. But when Adam and Eve sinned for the first time, it created a problem God needed to solve. There were seemingly contradictory truths at odds with each other. God's Holiness says that He could not come near sin, and death is the penalty for sin. (see Romans 6:23) God's Righteousness means that the penalty must be paid. (see Romans 8:1). God's Mercy says people cannot pay the price on their own. God's Love and Grace says, "I'll come to earth and pay it Myself" (see John 15:13).

Jesus came as a humble servant to live a perfect life, so He could show us the way to live righteously. He then died and rose to eternal life as the solution to those contradictory truths.

Why was Jesus the ONLY Possible Savior?

When I was a kid, I thought that "Christ" was Jesus's last name. In my world, people had two names: a first name and last name. In the Bible times, people and things were named for identifiable experiences. The word Christos or Christ means The ONE Anointed, the Deliverer, the Savior, the Messiah.

> John 3:16 (AMP) For God so loved the world that He gave His **only begotten** Son that whoever believes in Him will not perish but have eternal life.

In the Strong's Concordance, the term *only begotten* is *monogenés*[8]. It means unique, properly the one and only, its own kind, no other.

---

8 https://biblehub.com/str/greek/3439.htm Biblehub Greek lexicon search term "only begotten"

Jesus was 100% God and 100% man. In our math, that doesn't make sense. But it is not our math that matters. As we have already learned, Jesus was present at the very creation of the universe and all in it. Jesus shows up pre-incarnate as *The Angel of the Lord* 23 times in the Bible. [1] The Name *Son of God* was part of Jesus' identity.

Jesus was the only one in history who could have fulfilled the now known 353 biblical prophecies that were foretold in the Old Testament and confirmed in the New Testament.[2] Thanks to the biblical research done by Henry Parry Liddon[3] in the 1700's and continued and captured for you by the *According to the Scriptures* biblical scholars, you can check them out for yourself!

https://accordingtothescriptures.org/prophecy/353prophecies. html

Inspired by Parry Liddon's work, Professor of Mathematics, Dr. Peter Stoner wrote a book called *Science Speaks: Scientific Proof of the Accuracy of Prophecy in the Bible* in 1969.[4] Dr. Stoner identified that Jesus fulfilled the 24 prophecies in the last 24 hours of his life. He did a mathematical calculation of the likelihood of one person fulfilling just **eight** of those prophecies.

To understand the magnitude of that reality, Dr. Stoner gave this illustration: cover the entire state of Texas (268,820 square miles) with silver dollars up to two feet deep. The total number of silver dollars needed would be 10 to the 17th power. Next, mark one silver dollar so it can be easily identified and put it back. Then thoroughly stir all the silver dollars all over the state. Finally, blindfold someone and tell them they can travel anywhere that they want in Texas, but they must pick up only one silver dollar. The chance of finding that one marked silver dollar in a 2-foot deep pile covering the entire state of

Texas would be the same statistical chance for **just eight** prophecies coming true in one man. [5]Excerpt from Clips that Move Mountains.

When I was writing my first book, *Clips that Move Mountains,* I found this incredible clip from Echoing Praise ministries that still says it better than I could with my own words. http://bit.ly/1btqSOH[9]

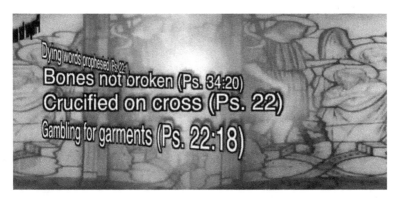

One of the things that I found interesting about these prophecies was the specificity of them. They were not generalized statements that could have been said about anyone. These were incredibly. Since Dr. Stoner did the math based on eight prophecies, let's look at eight very specific fulfilled prophecies from Jesus' life:

- *Sold for 30 pieces of silver*; forecasted Zechariah 11:12 and fulfilled in Matthew 26:14-15

- *His hands and feet were pierced* forecasted Psalm 22:16 and fulfilled in Luke 23:33 and John 20:25-27

- *His garments were divided, and lots cast for them* forecasted Psalm 22:18 and fulfilled John 19:24

9 Echoing Praise Ministries http://www.echoingpraise.com/video Prophetic Proof on Youtube: http://bit.ly/1btqSOH

- *His side was pierced* forecasted Zechariah 11:1, 12:10-12 and fulfilled in John 19:34-37

- *Buried in a rich man's tomb* forecasted Isaiah 53:9 and fulfilled in Matthew 27:57-60

- *Born in Bethlehem* forecasted Micah 5:2 and fulfilled in Matthew 2:1

- *Born of a virgin* forecasted Isaiah 7:14 and fulfilled in Matthew 1:18

- *Resurrected from the dead* forecasted Psalm 16:10-11; 49:15 and fulfilled in Mark 16:6

Even more remarkable is that some of these prophetic messages were between four hundred and fifteen hundred years before Jesus was even born.

Jesus' preferred Name for Himself was the *Son of Man.* Jesus chose to lay aside His deity and truly live tuned entirely into the Heavenly Father by the power of the Holy Spirit. He did this to show us how to do it. This is the truth of our capability when the Holy Spirit came to dwell in us.

What Does Salvation Include?

Most people associate the word "saved" to avoiding the eternal destination of hell and damnation. This is believing salvation is limited to the next life. Heaven is only part of what salvation means. It is for here and now too.

The Greek word sózó, [10] "to save" in the original Bible transcripts means to rescue, deliver from danger, heal, to restore, make well.

---

10   https://biblehub.com/greek/4982.htm Biblehub Greek lexicon search term "saved" and "deliverer"

The word *sōtḗ* refers to the deliverer, properly the ONE who brings salvation and makes us whole, healed, and delivered. This is also for the word Christos in the Greek or Christ.

The most important lesson here is that when you accept Jesus Christ as your Savior, you *have* eternal life. That means you are healed, delivered, and restored now. You don't have to wait until you are in heaven to experience your salvation. This truth includes both justification and sanctification.

Justification is your positioning in Christ. Once you are saved, you are a child of God, and you have your inheritance accessible now and in heaven. It's like you are at the right train station and have a ticket to the right train.

Many think that this ticket gets redeemed when they die. People imagine meeting Saint Peter at the gates of heaven and handing him their ticket. Then he lets them into heaven where they can finally enjoy peace and happiness. They live their entire lives believing the lie that they are wretched sinners and that they simply need to wait out this life to get their heavenly reward for saying "yes." But that is not the truth of what is available for you at salvation.

Sanctification is working out the Biblical truths of salvation daily. It is walking out the reality that you can board that train now. Eternal life begins at the moment of salvation. There is no need for you to live like you don't have the ticket now. Sanctification entails a daily process of confession, repentance and seeking God's face. Ask the Holy Spirit to continually guide and move you along the journey of Christian maturity, one day at a time. We will address this more fully in the Immanuel Chapter.

The Assurance of your Salvation

I believe that a lot of unsaved people think they are saved. Salvation is not an issue for which you want to be unsure. Let's look at what happens at the point of salvation, so you can be assured of your spiritual condition.

> Mark 16:16 [16] Whoever believes and is baptized will be saved, but whoever does not believe will be condemned.

The word here for *"believes" in the Bible is pistis.[11]* which means faith to believe, the persuasion of and from God. It is the divine spark of the gift of faith required for salvation. This belief is necessary to have the trust needed to accept Jesus into your heart. It is when you choose to lay aside your own will and grab hold of God's preferred will by His power. This relational agreement is a spiritual heart contract entered into at the point of salvation. Once that heart contract is made, your salvation is sealed, and it cannot be lost.

There is another word for "believe" in the Bible that needs to be looked at as well. Apisteó [12] is a belief that comes from man's own mind or disbelief in God's promises. An example would be a belief in a negative outcome or the lies of the enemy. The Strong's definition for this word is "to believe for self-serving reasons, without sacred meaning, to disbelieve, be faithless."

I have a student who shared a story of how he went through the motions of saying the salvation prayer to impress a girl in college. His motivation was to continue dating her and not because he genuinely believed in Christ. This action did not secure his salvation. Many years later, he had his real salvation encounter with the Lord and gave his heart entirely to God.

---

11 https://biblehub.com/str/greek/4103.htm Biblehub Greek lexicon search "believe"
12 https://biblehub.com/str/greek/569.htm Biblehub Greek lexicon search "disbelief"

Let's address the word "baptized" in Mark 16:16. The word for baptized in the Bible is *baptizó.* It refers to a submersion of water symbolizing the submersion in the Living Water of the Holy Spirit. To be baptized in the sense of Mark 16:16 is a display of a spiritual submersion. It is a surrendering your own will and rising to the will of God. This heart posture is demonstrated by the physical display of total submersion water baptism as your outward declaration of an internal spiritual commitment. The outward display of water baptism is not what is required here as much as the heart posture of submission that the ceremony represents.

Salvation is not ensured because you were born in a Christian home, baptized as a baby, raised with the Name of Jesus uttered in the household, or attended Bible classes. Each person needs to come to that humbling place on their own, and it is in the surrendering of your own will that the Lord gives you the gift to believe. There will be evidence in the life of someone truly saved.

Understanding the Newness of Salvation

Salvation brings many levels of new blessings into your life. You have a new life, a new relationship with God, a new identity, and new capability. Let's dive into each one.

New Life...New Wineskin

Jesus conquered sin and death so we can have eternal life now and live free from the bondage of sin, sickness, and the limitations of this world. (See Mark 16:16-17, and 2 Corinthians 5:17) your old self that is your sin nature was crucified on the cross with Jesus. He didn't just die for you, He died as you.

Because you have accepted Jesus, you have eternal life now and in heaven. You are free from the bondage of this world. You no longer have to accept illness or struggles as insurmountable challenges in your life. We've already learned that part of the definition of salvation or sózó includes healing. In Book 2 Encountering the HEALING of God, you will discover that God's healing is physical, mental, emotional, and spiritual.

Your heavenly accommodations will depend on how much you practice the truths of your salvation while you're still on earth. There is a connection between your life now and your life in heaven. Walking in alignment with the Lord, living out your freedom, healing, and victory, bearing much fruit for the Kingdom, will prove advantageous in your heavenly eternity. This is important to understand as this life is comparably like a single grain of sand on the shores of the entire world.

I asked the Lord to explain the parable of new wine and new wineskins.

> Mark 2:22 (AMP) [22] No one puts new wine into old [a] wineskins; otherwise the [fermenting] wine will [expand and] burst the skins, and the wine is lost as well as the wineskins. But new wine must be put into new wineskins."

> *The inside of an old wineskin could not be seen. Wine leaves behind a fermented residue as the wine ages. After the bottle has been open for a few days, the wine begins to ferment and turn sour many days after being opened? It is because it's starting to break down and rot. New wine poured into an old wineskin that has old rotting cells making the wine rotten. Molecules expand and burst the old wineskin.*

> *The new wineskin represents the new man, healed and untainted. The new wine stands for the truth of My Presence,*

My Grace, that comes with salvation; the Holy Spirit in fullness in your heart. When the believer agrees with the truth that they are free to live without the barriers or hindrances of the old sin nature, their heart is a new wineskin.

New Relationship...Direct Access to the Father

Before salvation, you and God were separate entities. You could always hear God because you have the eyes and ears of your heart. He was always there watching over you because of his Omnipresence. When Adam and Eve sinned, it separated us from the Father. Jesus covers us with His perfection, which gains us direct access to the Father. We can come right into God's presence and connect with His mind, will, and emotion. (See Hebrews 10:19-22)

The Holy of Holies was the place where God's Presence on earth resided. Only the High Priest once a year after major purification could go in that room to pray for God's atonement of sins for the people. At the moment that Jesus died on a cross, there was an earthquake and the veil covering the doorway to the Holy of Holies was ripped from top to bottom. Jesus had gained all believers direct access to the Heavenly Father in that moment.

Matthew 27:50-51 (AMP) "[50] When Jesus had cried out again in a loud voice, He yielded up His spirit. [51] At that moment the veil of the temple was torn in two from top to bottom. The earth quaked, and the rocks were split."

The size and thickness of the veil ensured that no one would accidentally fall into the Holy of Holies. The veil was 60 feet long, 30 feet wide, was one inch thick. It was so massive and heavy it took 300 priests to manipulate it. Notice that the temple curtain was torn from the top down to the bottom by God directly. What no human could possibly tear by human strength, God did by the death of the Son of God.

Jesus' finished work on the cross paid the penalty for Adam and Eve's original sin. Now we can go behind the curtain and have access to God directly. We have the confidence to enter the holy places by the blood of Jesus (Heb 10:19). [6] Jesus died and was resurrected not just to gain us access to heaven and to wash away our sins, but to give us direct access to God. The divine transaction made at the cross allows us to commune with God any time we want.

New Identity

When you accept the gift of salvation, you become an adopted son or daughter of God. With this new familial designation, there is a great inheritance.

> Galatians 3:26-28 (AMP) [26] For you [who are born-again have been reborn from above—spiritually transformed, renewed, sanctified and] are all children of God [set apart for His purpose with full rights and privileges] through faith in Christ Jesus. [27] For all of you who were baptized into Christ [into a spiritual union with the Christ, the Anointed] have clothed yourselves with Christ [that is, you have taken on His characteristics and values]. [28] There is [now no distinction in regard to salvation] neither Jew nor Greek, there is neither slave nor free, there is neither male nor female; for you [who believe] are all one in Christ Jesus [no one can claim a spiritual superiority].

I remember taking a Beth Moore class called *The Inheritance* many years ago. One thing I remember about it was the there are three major things we receive when we are adopted in the family of God; Presence, Property and People.

The Galatians verse reveals the Presence of God with the truth that we are united with Him and share His nature. This is what we are learning how to enjoy with the encounters that we are having with God's Names.

The physical Promised Land was the property of the inheritance in the days if the Old Testament, while today our property is our fruit bearing. We are set apart to accomplish God's purposes with full rights and privileges. This means He calls and equips us to do our Kingdom work and we earn rewards in heaven for it when we are in glory.

The people refer to how the Lord unites the body of Christ to come along side and help each other in accomplishing His purposes. As we will learn in the Book 3 *How to Encounter the DIRECTION of God*, our callings require God to orchestrate teams of people to help us along the way in a beautiful intertwining puzzle. Each piece has its own shape and size, all connecting to make one big Kingdom plan.

New Capability

All born-again believers have the power to exercise the Gifts of the Spirit.

> Mark 16:17 (AMP) [17] "These are the miraculous signs that **will** accompany believers: They **will** use the power and authority of My name to force demons out of people. They **will** speak new languages. [18] They **will** pick up snakes, and if they drink any deadly poison, it will not hurt them. They **will** place their hands on the sick and cure them."

This verse doesn't say that some believers will do these miraculous things. It says that believers will do these things. This means that we have the **capability** to do these things. Once saved, we have the

Holy Spirit in our hearts in fullness and as we grow in our spiritual maturity, He releases those capabilities to exercise those gifts.

When you step out in obedient faith by God's power you show God spiritual maturity and He trusts you with more. The book of James is all about this truth. James is saying that you will know a true believer because they are releasing God's power. They are not doing these things in their own strength because they are miraculous signs. Rather, by doing miraculous things, it proves that God lives within them.

> James 2: 14 (AMP) [14]What use is it, my brethren, if someone says he has faith but he has no works? Can that faith save him?

Get on the Train

If you are not sure if you have a salvation ticket, this chapter's encounters will allow you to settle that issue with Jesus directly. The Appendix has a salvation prayer. You can say whatever words God puts on your heart. Jesus will talk you through it! Once you have your ticket, you have eternal life! Get on that train now.

Your train ticket never expires. It's like a forever pass. Maybe you got on the train when you accepted Christ, but you are living below the victorious life that God wants for you. At some point, you got off the train. I did too when I lived my season of backsliding. Think of your ticket as a tattoo that God can always see. You can't lose it once you have it!

Trains go only one direction at a time. They don't go off on bunny trails of distraction. If you allow the Lord to be the Train Engineer, He will get you there! Meeting Immanuel next is a great way to find out how to stay on that train! Jesus is ready to take you to your destiny. Are you ready to get on that train?

Remember earlier when I said that one of the things that you are saved from is yourself? Forget every religious assumption you thought you knew, come to Jesus as a child and let Him show you the way Himself. Ask Him all your questions. Go to Him first!

Encountering the Savior:

Experience the Resurrection Encounter-https://bit.ly/30R6esw

Steps for this encounter:

- Welcome and thank God for His Presence and what He is about to share with you,

- Close your eyes and reflect on the events of the last week of Jesus' life…

- Picture Him riding on the colt through Jerusalem…

- See Him talking to the disciples about His body and His blood at the last supper…

- See Him praying at the garden of Gethsemane… and the soldiers taking Him away…

- See Him getting whipped and beaten…

- See Him on the cross, bleeding, and suffering…

- Now you are in a pitch-dark cave, you cannot see anything, but the room feels small. You feel the cold and dampness and realize you are inside the grave tomb of Jesus. You still can't see anything, but you smell the burial spices…

- Suddenly, the room is filled with bright light. You see the mummified body of Jesus. The layers of cloth strips and anointing spices binding His body. To your left and behind you, you see two more stone beds carved into the cave.

- Then, you see a curious sparking light like diamonds flashing in the bright light. It begins at His head and moves like a scanner over His entire body.

- You see a holographic image of Jesus begin to sit up through the clothes, and as He does, the mummy cloths fall to the stone bed underneath Him. He turns and begins to stand, and before your eyes, He solidifies and is standing in front of you. He took the strips that bound His head and folded them neatly and placed them separately from the rest of the burial fabric.

He smiles and winks at you and calls you by name.

- He waves to sit with you on the grave bed behind you.

- He is so happy to share this moment with you! While you sit with Him, a wave of love washes over you. You will have time to talk with Him here for a few minutes.

- When He is ready, He will stand up, wave His hand,roll the stone away, and walk out of the burial cave.

Before He does, ask Him these two questions:

- Lord, why were you willing to go through all of this? AND Lord, why did you do it for ME? Then dedicate or rededicate your life to Him. In your own words, pour out your heart's intention to follow Him carefully.

The Great Exchange Meet Jesus in your special place as a child. Spend some time playing with Him and then ask, "Lord, help me better understand how I can cooperate with the truths of the great exchange of your salvation."

Baptism of the Holy Spirit- https://bit.ly/2PMCQ0n

Steps for this Encounter

- Posture your heart a bit before this one. Listen to at least three praise and worship songs.

- Meet Jesus in your Special Place and ask Him to take you to the upper room on the day of Pentecost.

- Then read and meditate on Acts 2:1-4, pausing to visualize each piece. Experience it with Jesus.

Acts 2: 1-4 (AMP) [1] When the day of [a]Pentecost had come, they were all together in one place, (*See the faces of all the people. Look around this room and take in all the faces. People of every tribe and nation are in this room*).

[2] and suddenly a sound came from heaven like a rushing violent wind, and it filled the whole house where they were sitting. (*Hear and feel this mighty wind*).

[3] There appeared to them tongues resembling fire, which were being distributed [among them], and they rested on each one of them [as each person received the Holy Spirit]. *Jesus gives you one of these tongues of fire.*

[4] And they were all filled [that is, diffused throughout their being] with the Holy Spirit *(feel the sensation of the Holy Spirit filling you)*

85

And began to speak in other [b]tongues (different languages), as the Spirit was giving them the ability to speak out [clearly and appropriately]. (*allow your tongue to cooperate with the syllables the Holy Spirit is speaking through you. Listen to the room filled with so many languages*).

Praise and honor God for this experience and make sure you journal it!

[1] Biblegateway.com exact word search entire Bible term "the angel of the Lord"

[2] https://accordingtothescriptures.org/prophecy/353prophecies.html

[3] *The works of Henry Parry Liddon* Compilation article by Anglican Avenue history HTTP://Anglican history.org/Liddon/list.HTML

[4] Peter Stoner, *Science Speaks: Scientific Proof of the Accuracy of Prophecy in the Bible 107* (Chicago, Moody Press, 1969)

[5] Sadallah, Dr. Patty, *Clips that Move Mountains 2nd Edition* pages 41-42 Ingram Spark (2019)

[6] Source: https://faithinthenews.com/3-facts-temple-veil/

More of You by Colton Dixon

https://bit.ly/3iEhKxL

Meet Immanuel

O'come O' Come Immanuel. This Christmas song is our typical association with this Name of God. We see the wondrous miracle that God sent His Son as a helpless baby to live a sinless life. Jesus became the perfect sacrifice for our sins so we could draw near to the Father. One of the coolest Jesus encounters I've ever had was getting to experience what the shepherds did on the night of Jesus' birth.

It was a creative writing class assignment for my Doctoral program. I was to experience and write about a Bible story from two perspectives. It was close to Christmas, and most of the songs reference the baby Jesus and the shepherds. So, I was excited to do this exercise using this Bible story. I experienced it as myself observing unseen, much like Ebenezer Scrooge did in *A Christmas Carol* by Charles Dickens. The second perspective was through the eyes of a shepherd. You can experience the miracle with me and gain a fresh appreciation for the meaning of the season now and every Christmas season. See Appendix D, Shepherds Two-Ways.

Three Ways God is With Us

The Name Immanuel means God is with us. God always was, is, and always will be with us. This is God's omnipresence, self-existing outside of time and space. In our natural world, this is hard for us to comprehend.

Everything that has ever happened or will happen has already happened for God. Every moment of your life, God has been with you including your future. This is true whether a person accepts Christ as their Savior or not. God knowing what we will do doesn't mean that we are puppets being controlled by Him. He has given us free will, which is why there is so much mess in the world. But He takes no one captive. People must come to Him willingly.

He knows what we are going to do because He has seen us do it. That's why there could be 353 fulfilled prophecies. He saw it happen already. You can trust that His Bible promises will come true. The interesting thing about the truth of God's omnipresence is that he can be *more there* at certain times than at others. God is more there for you when you are fixing your eyes on Him.

The most common way to think of the name Immanuel is associated with Jesus coming to earth as a human and living among us for 33 years. Jesus lived to show us how to bring to life the truths of the Bible, to bring us back to the Father, to conquer sin and death, and bring us to eternal life now and in heaven. He showed us how to live totally tuned into the Holy Spirit because we are adopted children of the King of Kings and citizens of Heaven.

When Jesus sent the Holy Spirit to dwell in our hearts, His capability multiplied by a million fold. This explains the verse below.

He is not saying that because you are a believer, you are better than Him. He is saying that He is multiplied in the hearts of believers so all of us can be releasing Him in the world. When He was a man, He was limited by the geography of his physical body. Now He is in all of us, all over the world!

> John 14:12 (AMP) [12] I assure you and most solemnly say to you, anyone who believes in Me [as Savior] will also do the things that I do, and He will do even greater things than these [in extent and outreach] because I am going to the Father.

Immanuel is the name of the God that walks with you every day and shows you how to live totally tuned to the Father naturally supernatural so you can release God's love and kingdom purposes to the world, for which you have influence. This is the most critical aspect of Immanuel for you to understand.

Justification vs. Sanctification

When we met the Savior, we became born again into the family of God and learned about justification. Justified means that our accepting Christ allowed us to meet the standard to be considered righteous in God's eyes. This is when God adopts us into His family.

> Galatians 2:20 (AMP) [20] I have been crucified with Christ [that is, in Him I have shared His crucifixion]; it is no longer I who live, but Christ lives in me. The life I now live in the body I live by faith [by adhering to, relying on, and completely trusting] in the Son of God, who loved me and gave Himself up for me.

Justification by salvation is a one-time deal. You can't screw up and lose your salvation. You are sealed for all time.

> 2 Corinthians 1:21-22 (AMP) [21] Now it is God who establishes and confirms us [in joint fellowship] with you in Christ, and who has anointed us [empowering us with the gifts of the Spirit]; [22] it is He who has also put His seal on us [that is, He has appropriated us and certified us as His] and has given us the [Holy] Spirit in our hearts as a pledge [like a security deposit to guarantee the fulfillment of His promise of eternal life].

Walking out the truths and realities of that new relationship and positioning is called sanctification. That is your part in cooperating with the indwelling Spirit to align yourself with God's best plans for you. This is a one day at a time job of abiding in Christ.

> John 15:4-5 (AMP) [4] Remain in Me, and I [will remain] in you. Just as no branch can bear fruit by itself without remaining in the vine, neither can you [bear fruit, producing evidence of your faith] unless you remain in Me. [5] [a]I am the Vine; you are the branches. The one who remains in Me and I in him bears much fruit, for [otherwise] apart from Me [that is, cut off from vital union with Me] you can do nothing.

The truth of this reality is critical to whether you will live a life of bondage or freedom. In Romans 7, Paul rants about how he wants to do the right thing but always seems to be doing the wrong thing. He tries and tries and just can't seem to get it together (See all of Romans 7).

This is us when we don't realize the truth of our salvation and inheritance of the indwelling Holy Spirit. In Romans 8, Paul teaches us we have the Spirit of the Life of Christ Jesus to overcome all of our issues. Abiding in Christ and surrendering to God are the secrets to victory in all areas (See all of Romans 8).

How to Abide in Christ

I asked the Lord to give me a metaphor to help me understand the principle of abiding in Christ.

> *Things plugged into the electricity can perform as designed. Those same things unplugged will lay dormant, unable to accomplish what they were created to do.*

Then the Lord showed me an image of the flux capacitor from the *Back to the Future* movies.[13] This image reminded me of the Father, Son, and Holy Spirit pulsing energy to me, and for my need to connect to God for that energy. When I received this image, it cracked me up that the Lord would speak to me with such a cultural reference. I looked up the words. Flux means continuous flow, and capacitor means two-way electrical energy. This is what He had to say about it: See this short clip from the movie: https://youtu.be/HyWqxkaQpPw

> *See the energy of the flux capacitor? It continuously pulses toward the center. You have the privilege of being connected to the energy of the Trinity – God's perfect will and power. Stay plugged in!*

---

13 Film clip from Back to the Future Movie on Youtube https://youtu.be/HyWqxkaQpPw

The source of My power is endless and always available. Always learn to stay plugged into it, so you don't miss a single blessing. The more energy you get from Me, the more you will reflect Me to those I have given you to serve. You were created in My image to reflect Me to the world. This is what you can do when you stay connected.

You stay plugged in by keeping your eyes fixed on Me. When I am in front of your mind, you will always include Me in all things. When you pull away from Me, you pull the plug and will disconnect from My power source. Just like an object that relies on electricity to function, you are dead, impotent in your effectiveness. Don't let this happen because it leaves you vulnerable to the enemy and keeps you from accomplishing what I desire.

Always seek Me to plug in. Your fruit will reveal whether you are connected or disconnected. The law of the Spirit of Christ Jesus is the energizing power that you sense when you fix your eyes on Me- the One who lives in you –you will receive rhema, (My spoken words to you) and vision as long as you follow in fellowship with the Holy Spirit.

Remember this metaphor about electricity. The Law of the Spirit of Christ Jesus is this electricity. It is your energy for life in Me. Staying connected gives you all My strength to live according to My perfect plan for you.

When you tune into the flow, you will know My heart and My will. You will have increased clarity of how I I want you to serve. I share my heart with you through images, thoughts, and feelings. Let us reason together; live this life with Me.

Four Rules of Abiding

To abide is to dwell. The synonyms for dwell are to stay, live, inhabit, settle and reside. When you learn how to abide in Christ, you begin to live the naturally supernatural life God created you to live. Game rules show you how to play and win. These are the rules for effective abiding in Christ.

Abiding leads to an increasing of God's anointing. The Bible word for anointing is *chrió*[14]. It means a smearing of the material Presence of God that sticks on you and empowers you to accomplish God's purposes. God's anointings come in many different forms and we will address many of them in this book and the others in this series.

Welcome the Holy Spirit

To be welcomed is to be included. When you leave the Holy Spirit behind for most of your day, you're not making Him feel welcome. Remember, He is always there, Involving Him in all aspects of your life will help Him feel appreciated. Many people believer that God is too busy for the little things I your life. This is a limiting lie. God dwells in your heart always and is waiting for you to engage Him. I honestly believe that He gets the most delight when we include Him for the small things. It's easy to cry out to God when you are in a crisis, but when you simply thank Him for that parking spot He's elated.

Fix your eyes on Jesus

Worry is nothing more than fixing your eyes on your problems and not on the truth of who God is in each circumstance. What you fix your eyes on grows within you. If you fix your eyes on your fears or negative outcomes, you set in motion that self-fulfilling prophecy.

The goal is to become more aware of where your eyes are fixed. Looking at your circumstance through your eyes will limit your

---

14 https://biblehub.com/greek/5548.htm Bible search term 'to anoint'

understanding to present information. When seeing things through the enemy's lens , you will only see negative outcomes. But when you look through Jesus' eyes, you are able to see things from His Omni perspective.

Ask the Lord to show you His heart for people or circumstances and He will shift your perspective to align with His. This is how to find the peace that surpasses understanding.

Become more Spirit Conscious

The more time you spend with someone gives you a greater sense of who they are and what you can expect from them. You know who you can trust by time spent with them. The same is true when abiding with Christ. The more time you spend with God, the more you will know His voice.

Pay attention to the spontaneous thoughts you receive when you are communing with God and test them against what you know to be true about God. Asking the questions; is that true? Or does this sound like God's names, character, promises, or nature? Or, does it reflect the enemy's personality or nature? Am I too analytical or logical? Or am I limiting my thoughts to this natural world? The more time you spend with God, the more discerning you become about which voice you are hearing.

Speak in Agreement

Abiding in Christ leads to transformation. The Lord created the heavens and the earth by speaking them into existence. We were created in His image. When you speak out loud what the Lord has revealed to you, it activates your faith. I found an increased boldness and anointing when I began sharing what I was learning from the Lord with others. Our God is a God of multiplication!

> James 3:17 (AMP) [17] But the wisdom from above is first pure [morally and spiritually undefiled], then peace-loving [courteous, considerate], gentle, reasonable [and willing to listen], full of compassion and good fruits. It is unwavering, without [self-righteous] hypocrisy [and self-serving guile].

The courage to speak what the Lord reveals takes you deeper in the abiding relationship with Christ. This boldness not only continues to grow your character, it shows the Lord that you can be trusted with His anointing.

Let Go of the "I" Mentality

One day I asked the Lord to shed light on the most essential part of understanding this abiding relationship with Him. This is what He said:

> *You can't have it both ways. You can have the fullness of Me and hold onto the selfishness of you. If you keep Me as your focus, the emphasis always, then you will remain "in Me." Whenever the focus shifts back on you, it's a red flag that you are off track.*

> *If you feel yourself thinking or saying, "I'm trying," then you know you're not resting in Me. This lesson of focusing on Me is so critical to the abundant Christian life. Learn how to catch your "self" mode and redirect your focus back on Me. Remember, it's is a process. This is countercultural, so be patient with yourself. You are on the path to living an abiding lifestyle. Once it becomes your more natural focus, it becomes much easier.*

Your prayers need to continue to change. Pray more of "God's will be done" rather than for what you want and how you want it. You will get there!

For more on how to pray God's prayers and not your own, see The Appendix A Dialogue Journaling Tips section called How to Pray without an Idol in Your Heart.

Lessons about Striving and Resting

Getting ahead of God and striving were major issues the Lord needed to address with me. I remember precisely when and how I learned these lessons.

Truth at Work is a national ministry that helps people learn how to surrender their businesses to God. I was at a point in my life where I felt I needed to focus my work on God completely. I had over 30 years of experience as an organization development consultant for faith-based nonprofits. This meant that I helped teams, and organizations plan for their futures with strategic planning, team development, training, facilitation, and coaching.

At that time in my life, I did not realize that God anoints all surrendered work to Him. You don't have to have a formal ministry to serve God. When the opportunity for the Regional Director position for *Truth at Wor*k opened for me in Ohio, I was sure this position was for me. After all, it was right up my skill set, and I knew exactly how I would do it!

While that two-year season of my life did bring me some lessons and blessed those involved, it was hard work! It did not come easy for me to enroll people to participate in it. I spent more time struggling to find people to join in that service than I did delivering it. It was a painstaking uphill battle.

Ray Hilbert, the founder of *Truth at Work* kept asking me, "Are you absolutely sure that God directed you to this role?" The question offended me! After all, it was right up my skill set, and I knew exactly how I would do it! But if I was honest with myself, I assumed the opportunity was mine, and I never asked God about it.

Two years into the ministry, I was diagnosed with Lyme's disease. I talked to Ray Hilbert about wanting to take off six months for my healing season. He released me from the role. He felt like it was too difficult for me, and he wanted to give me a way out.

Within two weeks of my stepping away from that work, the Lord gave me the downloaded assignment to write *Clips That Move Mountains.* On some levels, it was easier to surrender to the Lord for this project because I had never written a book before. This book included film clips that I would write about as biblical metaphors for the discipleship journey to the abundant Christian life. I had been writing clip-based blog articles for some time for my ministry business. But I had never seen a book with film clips before, and I assumed things that cost me five months delay.

I assumed that because there were film clips in the book, I would need permission to use them. The Lord would inspire me to write something about a film clip, and then I would ask permission, and people would say no. The truth is, He never told me I needed to request permission. One day in frustration, I was crying out to the Lord about it, and He said:

> *If I inspire you to write about a clip, write it. I never told you that permission was necessary. Just write the book!*

So, I wrote the book. The Lord directed me to send a draft of the book to the film clip companies represented in it. He wanted me to make sure they understood this was not a permissions draft. It was an opportunity for them to partner with me on this project. I sent the draft, and I waited.

A short time later, I received an envelope from Universal Studios with a cease and desist threat in it. I freaked out. I asked the Lord what I was supposed to do about it. He directed me to a Christian Fair Use lawyer. It turns out there are five different ways media can be used without permission. Only one was required to earn 'free-use' status. My book project hit all five. I never needed any permission. My lawyer sent back the fair use law letter to Universal Studios, and I never heard from them again.

My lessons in the season were: 1. God knows everything. 2. His timing is always perfect. 3. Things are more of a struggle and take longer if I take matters into my own hands. 4. Trusting God is the fastest way to accomplish anything He gives you to do. 5. The quicker you learn how to rest and not strive, the more effectively you will accomplish the goals and plans that God has for you.

Here is a picture of the level of resting the Lord wants for you.

The Lord showed me a rubber ducky on a creek. It was going along the stream quickly guided by the water. By itself, it had no power without the forces of the river. The river represents the river of Living Water which is the Holy Spirit's powerful guidance in your heart.

How much power did the rubber ducky contribute to its journey?

None, Lord.

This is the level of trust and surrender that I desire for you. I navigate the waters, not you. I know you are concerned about the issues of this life. This is the lesson you must learn in all aspects of your life: what you eat and drink, what you do, what you work on, and your relationships. Don't be tempted to take matters into your own hands. If you want victory in all areas, you need to let Me do the driving.

There are missed blessings when you shut Me out, even if unintentionally. But you don't get there by trying harder. You get there by letting go, taking your hands off the wheel of your life and trusting Me with it. I'm the blanket that covers your whole life. It's not like departments where you have control of some, and I have control of others. Control is a myth. I am in control of everything except your free will to cooperate with Me. Releasing your notion of control is the secret to resting and not striving.

Remember to let go, be still, cease striving and relax and know that I am God (Psalm 46:10. The more you know Me, each characteristic of Me, the easier it will be for you to live out that verse.

Order My Day

To activate these lessons in abiding, the Lord taught me an important lesson about the Holy habit of having Him order my day.

Me first, Me first, Me first.

I would hear this in my spirit whenever I would get up and go without first spending time with God. I observed that when I did spend the first fruits of my time with God, my day went well. When I left God behind, I would have frustrating days. But when I began thanking and praising God even before my eyes were fully open, it set my heart posture for the entire day.

I learned that this focused attention on God was like filling up my spiritual gas tank. I would see and sense His guidance and direction more and my productivity went through the roof.

> *Ask Me to order your day. I know what you are up against today, so trust Me. If I put something on your list, do it. If I don't put it on your list, it's not for today. When you only do what I have put on your list and keep an open heart for the surprises for the day, you will remain under My covering and anointing.*

Each day I spend time with God praising and worshiping, then I sit down to my journal and we chat about the day. Somedays He puts a lot on my list and I'm amazed that at the end of the day I got all of it done. Other day, it's a small list and I get calls from people who need ministry. I never look at those calls as a disruption to my day. It's God's day and I am simply living it for Him.

There is no greater secret to high performance than being under the anointed power of God! We will address this in greater detail in Book 3 *Encountering the DIRECTION of God.*

Being in His Skin

One day, at our Spirit Life Circle, we had a wonderful discussion about what it means to be IN Christ. The group spent 15 minutes journaling that question. We were asking the Lord to shed more light on its meaning. I went to the bathroom before I started the journaling exercise at the coffee shop, where there is a full-length mirror.

Turning and looking in the mirror, I saw myself, but I also saw Jesus. He was holographically over me, covering me. I could see me, and I could see Him. Instantly, I journaled that experience. And the Lord said;

This vision is the spiritual Truth. There is no intervention needed to step into My skin when you realize you are always in My skin. This is the truth of the new man; the Life of the Spirit in Christ Jesus referred to in Romans chapter 8.

See yourself with Me covering you. We are ONE ALL the time. My Power, Presence, Nature, and Wisdom are always there. When you focus inward to your heart, you will always be able to tap into this Truth.

Place your palms face up and wiggle your fingers. Do you see My hands as well?

Yes, Lord. I see your hands, your fingers wiggling with mine, and I see the scars on your wrists.

Cross your legs, what do you see?

I see my leg crossed over my other leg. And I see Your robed leg crossed over it as well.

Practice this week, seeing Me covering you. When you wave your arms, when you take steps, and especially when you are challenged. Remember this truth that you do not need to step into My skin to see, hear, feel, and think My thoughts. But that you already are in My skin and you can access My thoughts, feelings, and character. This is an essential lesson in learning the abiding lifestyle, especially when struggling with sin or trials. I have overcome sin and death. IN ME, you have too!

The Holy Spirit is in your heart. When you release Him, you are seeing, hearing, feeling, and thinking His thoughts. The best way that I have found to understand the unity of the Christ-Identity is to practice seeing yourself as merged into Jesus as ONE. Becoming aware that you can be and, in fact, always are *in His skin* will more quickly align you with Him. It is much easier to understand by experience than to explain, so your encountering exercises will get you there.

You need to increase your self-awareness of the genuine spiritual reality that you are IN CHRIST. To understand that Christ is in you is to agree that the Holy Spirit lives in fullness for you to access His mind, will and emotion by using the eyes and ears of your heart. Understanding and walking out these truths are the essence of successfully living the lifestyle of walking with Immanuel.

Encountering Immanuel

In His Skin – https://bit.ly/2FcUSXy

Steps for this Encounter

- Relax and breathe deeply. Thank Immanuel for what He is about to do for you.

- Go to your special place as a child and talk to Him about your most significant relationship challenge. Jesus will lead you to a memory with this person (you don't need to tell Him which one!)

- He will take you by the hand and pull you into His skin, so you can see, hear, feel, and think His thoughts about this relationship and situation.

- He will show you His heart for the situation, help you see through His eyes giving you His perspective on this person's heart and this circumstance.

- Allow this reframing to show you the way to reconcile and forgive this challenging person or circumstance.

- Have a conversation with Immanuel about what you just learned while you were in His Skin and ask Him what steps you can take now to improve this relationship.

- He knows what needs to happen and what to do, so trust Him in this. He will take it from there regarding next steps or instructions. Do this more than once if you find it helpful.

His Covering – https://bit.ly/3gYiP36

Steps for this Encounter

- Spend some time worshipping the Lord for a few minutes and thanking Immanuel for what He is about to show you.

- In the Spirit, imagine yourself standing before a full-length mirror.

- See yourself, but also see Jesus too. He is over you, like a hologram.

- Now step away from the mirror, and just look at your arms and legs.

- Wave your arms... see Him and you in perfect sync.

- Do you notice anything different about how you see, feel, think or hear things?

- Ask Him your questions about this Truth and especially what tips He has for you to remember.

- Ask Him to show you a picture or a metaphor to explain this true spiritual reality of you and He being united. He will explain it in your language.

- Journal out this entire experience.

- Remember to ask Him anything and thank Him for what He shows you!

- Practice simply noticing His covering on you at other times this week.

Order My Day

- This is more of a Holy Habit than a one-time encounter. It is a practice that will improve your abiding lifestyle with Immanuel.

- Each day spend time in Praise and Worship and in the Word of God. Prioritize your time with the Lord and give Him your first attention.

- Ask Him to tell you what He wants you to do today. He will show you the day's priorities. If you think you should be doing something and He has not put it on your list, you can ask Him why, but trust that He will have you get to it when He wants you to. If that is not today, that's OK.

- Obey Him and do what He has given you allowing for life's surprises. It is HIS day and He's not surprised by anything.

- At the end of the day, reflect on how your day went, how much you accomplished and if you noticed more of His anointing Presence.

- Make this a daily habit and you will be living the abiding lifestyle!

[1] Biblegateway.com biblical keyword search *The Angel of the Lord,* exact phrase parameter Genesis to Malachi in the Amplified Bible.

Beloved by Tenth Avenue North

https://bit.ly/30NTF1m

Meet the Bridegroom

⟨∂∕∕⟩

*O*f all the names of God, the Bridegroom is perhaps the most intimate and least understood. I first met the Bridegroom in 2007 when I took a class on the Song of Solomon and the Bridegroom's Heart when I was interning at the Cleveland House of Prayer. I had a powerful experience that I will share with you as one of our encounters at the end of this chapter. Part of our internship curriculum was to study Mike Bickle's work on the Song of Solomon. Mike Bickel from the International House of Prayer of Kansas City has made it his life work to understand this Name. To my knowledge, no one has done a more in-depth study of the Song of Solomon.[i]

The Lord gripped Bickle's heart in 1989 and gave him a life's mission to add the lens of the Song of Solomon to 24-hour music, prayer, and praise. Before 1989, he never studied the book or even heard anyone preach or teach on the subject.

Not a Gender Thing

One of the reasons the Song of Solomon is underrepresented in pulpits is that most people interpret it only as a story of physical love between Solomon and his Shulamite bride. Looking at this book through that single lens limits God's definition of this Name. It creates a gender-related resistance to the Bridegroom that is a barrier to a real revelational understanding and intimacy with God.

Song of Solomon is an allegory of the love between devoted followers representing the bride, and Jesus, the Bridegroom. The book addresses two major themes: trust and partnership. The Song of Solomon is essentially a story of the progression of a new believer becoming a heart-sick, sold out, fruit-bearing partner of God.

Even Bickle himself admits that he had to overcome gender assumptions at his initial reading of this book. He read it and was confused. Why would the Lord give him this book about kisses, breasts, gardens, and gushy lovey-dovey language? He was a man, not a bride. But the Lord kept on pressing and told him to stick with it. He would reveal its real meaning. The Lord kept on insisting... commanding.

"Read it again, read it again, read it again!"

By Spirit-led revelation, the Lord made it clear to Bickle that this book was not about gender or sex, as most assume. Rather, it is about the trust and partnership necessary for true fruit-bearing and co-reigning with Christ that the Scriptures promise.

> Revelation 3:21-22 Tree of Life Version (TLV) [21] To the one who overcomes I will grant the right to sit with Me on My throne, just as I Myself overcame and sat down with My Father on His throne. [22] He who has an ear, let him hear what the Ruach [Holy Spirit] is saying to Messiah's communities."

The Beginning of the Journey to Maturity

The Song of Solomon has two halves that mark out the believer's journey to spiritual maturity and fulfillment in Christ. In the first four-and one-half chapters the new believer, represented by the Shulamite lover, is learning the blessing of the Presence of God. Her focus is on all the wonderful and beautiful things that the Lord's Presence means for her.

In the first four verses of Chapter 1, the believer has just realized the beauty and blessing of being kissed by the kisses of her lover's mouth.

> Song of Solomon 1:2 (AMP) "May he kiss me with the kisses of his mouth!" [Solomon arrives, she turns to him, saying,] "For your love is better than wine.

This verse refers to meeting God on the pages of His Word (the kisses of His mouth) and realizing His love for us. New believers learn about the blessings of being in God's Presence. Her journey begins with what Bickle calls a Paradox of Grace.

> Song of Solomon 1:5 (AMP)"I am dark [in heart] but lovely [to God]...my own vineyard [heart] I have not kept.

The darkness is not related to skin color, but rather our imperfections, our sinful nature. The Lord meets us right where we are at salvation, warts and all. He doesn't need us to be anything more than who we are in that moment. He shows you He loves you as is. The verse reveals the areas of her heart that need repentance. God deals with those areas with gentle love, affection, comfort, and edification. You don't need to be anything more than you are for Him to want you.

Our focus at this stage is on all He can do for you. This is an immature beginning to the journey, but the Lord still loves you no less. However, God has much more for you and doesn't want to leave you there. So, He issues a test of conviction where He reveals your heart and causes you to become repentant. This is not to punish you, but rather He lovingly corrects you and moves you forward. The goal of this divine correction is increasing faith, hope, and love.

At this stage in the believer's life, the hunger for God is awakened with a Holy dissatisfaction with current intimacy. Their heart cry is for MORE! This is what the Lord had to say about this truth.

> *I created everyone to cry for MORE, MORE, MORE! Their hearts desire more of Me. But the flesh can confuse that heart cry and desire MORE in the wrong direction. That's why there is so much idolatry and addictions in the world because I created you to want more. The challenge is to understand that true satisfaction and fulfillment come from Me, not anything or anyone else. The first challenge is discovering that what the heart actually wants, and needs is more of Me.*

> *It only takes a small taste of the real love of Me to move you. Experiencing that love can be more addictive than anything else. Encountering the "realness" of Me is the secret. Meeting more and more aspects of my Names and character is a way for you to increase this hunger for Me.*

> *My love is a holy addiction. A small taste of My love will increase your hunger for a bigger meal. Many never taste and see that I am good, so they don't know what they're missing. They try to fill the God-shaped hole in their hearts with more of whatever won't satisfy. Then they wonder why they are so unhappy.*

God loves you exactly as you are. We don't need to be good enough for Him to grip our hearts with His unmatchable love. He wants more for you. This is why He issues tests to show you your heart and causes you to become repentant.

> Song of Solomon 1:6 (AMP) Stop staring at me because I am so dark.
> The sun has tanned me.
> My brothers were angry with me.
> They made me the caretaker of the vineyards.
> I have not even taken care of my own vineyard.

She is aware of the sins in her heart and is agreeing that she has not taken care of her vineyard (her heart)., Responding in agreement with God's correction moves you to repentance and leads to purity of heart, faith, hope, and love. This is about you taking care of your own heart.

Serving in ministry without taking care of your heart is like a vineyard caretaker who has not taken care of his own garden. We cannot do things for God successfully without His power to do them. We cannot release what we don't have to give. Serving for God is actually apart from God. This kind of service can lead to burnout because it is coming from your own strength and not God's. The tests represented in Chapters 1 and 2 are about purifying.

> Isaiah 1:25 Names of God Bible (NOG) I will turn my power against you. I will remove your impurities with bleach. I will get rid of all your impurities.

God's gentle conviction is pointing out the areas in your heart that need to heal and be made whole. Sin patterns reveal areas of needed forgiveness. God puts a gentle finger on areas that need to be healed, purified, and released to Him. Passing the tests by confession and repentance bring you into a season of surrender and increased prioritization of God.

The Mountains

At the beginning of Song of Solomon Chapter 2, the bride is blissfully happy that she is receiving so much love from her lover. He is speaking life into her spirit, really helping her accept her worthiness and building her up with faith, hope, and love. Then, He issues a challenge for her to step out of her comfort zone.

> Song of Solomon Chapter 2:8-9 (AMP) [8] Behold, he is coming—
> leaping over the mountains,
> springing over the hills!
> [9] My lover is like a gazelle
> or a young buck among the stags.
> Look! He is standing behind our wall—
> gazing through the windows,
> peering through the lattice.
> [10] In response, my lover said to me:
> "Get yourself up, my darling,
> my pretty one, and come, come![a]
> [11] For behold, the winter has past; the rain is over, it has gone.
> [12] Blossoms appear in the land,
> the time of singing has come,
> and the voice of the turtle-dove
> is heard in our land.
> [13] The fig tree ripens its early figs.
> The blossoming vines give off their fragrance.
> Arise, come, my darling,
> my pretty one, and come, come!

Here God is saying, *I'm way up here, leaping effortlessly on mountains. Won't you come with Me and we can leap over the hills together?* He wants you to go with Him, so together, you will skip on the mountains. God's heart cry is for you to accept His invitation to step into a huge calling in an area of influence for which He has specifically designed for you. It's your unique part of God's fantastic plan. He is saying, I have amazing plans for us together, but I need you to come with Me!

Lance Wallnau has taught for many years about the 7 *Mountains of Cultural Influence.*[1] We will study this in-depth in the Book 3 *Encountering the DIRECTION of God.*

But I share it here because your Divine purpose is somewhere in the Kingdom plan of one or more of these mountains.

- **The Family**- foundationally influences emotional health and wellbeing of the person,

- **Media, Education and Arts & Entertainment** - Collectively influences and defines worldview, beliefs, and values

- **Government**- Interprets and enforces laws

- **Business**- affects prosperity and economy

- **Religion**- defines ideas about God, morality, and values.

  Deuteronomy 28:13 (AMP) [13] The Lord will make you the head (leader) and not the tail (follower), and you will be above only. You will not be beneath, if you listen and pay attention to the commandments of the Lord your God, which I am commanding you today, to observe them carefully.

When the Lord says, skip on mountains with Me, He is calling you to your divine purpose. Notice, that the verse does not say skip on mountains **for** Me, it says skip on mountains **with** Me. This is a crucial distinction to understand if you are going to pass this test.

The Comfort Zone Test

The second type of test is the one that separates the immature Christian from the mature one. The comfort zone test is about trusting God to go way beyond your natural abilities and dreams. The fear of losing your comfort in this challenge can be paralyzing. There's a thought in the back of your mind that says that a hundred percent obedience to God will be painful and be too costly for you to pay. For this reason, most people begin by saying no.

Saying No

> Song of Solomon 2:15 Catch the foxes for us— the little foxes that ruin the vineyards, for our vineyards are in blossom.

The foxes represent the distractions, busyness, and priorities for your time that you have made higher than God. These are the Shulamite's excuses for not going with Him to the mountains. Notice that the foxes ruin the vineyards. The vineyard represents your heart, and the fruit of the vine is your fruit-bearing or your effectiveness for Christ. The blossoms of the vineyard show that the harvest is ready. When God calls you to a higher challenge, He is saying the time is right for you to come with Him now.

Our destiny is to conquer the mountains with God. And He's not willing to leave us behind, so He lets us wrestle by quieting Himself. The Shulamite woman initially failed the comfort zone test. She was not ready to skip on the mountains with her beloved. She allowed her fears, and the foxes stop her. She was happy staying in her safe comfort zone. But her 'no' created a feeling of distance from her lover. Even though God is still as close as breathing, when you disobey, He feels distant. He has not left, but disobedience has created a static. It's hard to hear Him now. You may think God has moved, but it's you. He's right there, watching and listening and even praying on your behalf that you catch up to your calling.

The real reasons for saying no are fear and priorities. The fear comes from not really understanding that you are doing this with God and under His power and in partnership. We limit God when we think that the big calling is something we need to do in our own strength. So, initially, we say no to things like; taking that mission trip, writing a book, confronting and forgiving an abuser, going into business, completely changing your career, talking to that stranger in the Walmart, etc. We don't realize when we say no, we move outside of God's covering. The safest place we can be is under the umbrella of God's provision, power, and safety, which comes only from obedience.

Understand this truth; if the calling isn't scary and huge, it's not from God. He doesn't put small things on our hearts, because then we would be tempted to do them in our own strength. No, these are always big things! And He wants every single believer to say yes, Lord, send me!

Remove "Self" from the Equation

One of the main learning lessons at this stage of maturity is to learn how to give God "ALL" and remove "SELF" from the equation. This is what God said about this issue:

> *Removing "self" is a process of onion layers. Self-issues pop up in so many areas of life. Self-consciousness is essentially the*

117

fear of man's reaction, needing the approval of others and caring about what people think more than what I think.

Self-effort is when you think you don't need Me. This is a pervasive problem. I find people praying to Me only "when all else fails." The lie of self-sufficiency is a lie of unneed. Believing that you don't need Me has led many lives down the road to destruction, beginning with Adam and Eve at the beginning of time!

Selfishness is when you care about your own wants above the needs of others and, more importantly, My will. Selfishness is the opposite of love because it forsakes Me. Self-promotion is rooted in ego. It's principally serving yourself. You cannot serve two masters; you cannot serve yourself and Me.

To purpose in your spirit to give Me ALL is to decide to agree with Me. It is in your best interest because I am the Omni-God. I know everything, see everything, have sovereign control over everything, and I'm always love. It's acknowledging that I have Jeremiah 29:11 very best plans for you, and there is no better person to trust with your life than Me. My yoke is easy, and My burden is light.

Count the Cost

Another thing that Kingdom heroes had in common was that they were willing to pay any cost for the sake of Jesus. Most said no before they said yes, many arguing with God of their lack of qualifications! Moses begged God to choose someone else, sighting his language deficiencies. Jonah didn't say yes until God delivered him from the belly of the whale! This is what the Lord said about counting the cost:

There is always a cost of obedience. It will cause a sacrifice of time, personal will, and resources. Realizing that your life IS My life and your efforts are part of My plan is one of the first

118

steps to understanding that the cause of Christ is worth any expense. Your life is not your own; it was bought with a price. Every sacrifice you make is always a gain. Here on earth and in heaven, your "losses" can become your greatest rewards and blessings.

For those who give it all, who remain faithful until death, there is a Martyrs Crown that will bless them enormously for eternity. Oh, if people could see the eternal reward for this type of sacrifice, the world would be a better place! Most see the sacrifices as losses. There is always gain when you are willing to pay anything for My sake.

Sacrifice is the fruit of a heart of gratitude. Those with a grateful heart knows that you cannot out-give Me. They are in touch with the truth of salvation and the fullness of Christ in their hearts. Those hearts yearn to thank Me no matter what.

Everything is a TEST!

Whenever something challenging or difficult comes our way, we tend to pray for God to take it away. Not every lousy circumstance is necessarily from the enemy. Sometimes the Lord allows challenging things to happen so He can use them to bring you forth in spiritual maturity.

The more powerful choice is to thank God for the challenge and ask Him what you need to learn from it. Getting Lymes disease was not something I would wish on anyone, but the Lord turned that around and used it as my catapulting experience! I look back now on that season as the greatest gift of my life because it caused me to go deep in God's presence and find my Kingdom purpose.

Everything is a test! Every blessing, every challenge, every trial, and even every tragedy is an opportunity to learn a lesson that will draw you near to the heart of God. Once in His presence, He can use all those things to heal, purify, and transform you into your Christ-Identity. The sooner you recognize that you are experiencing a test, the more you can put on the clothes of God's righteousness and overcome it. Your life story is your gospel; your Jesus story lived out for His glory.

Crossing the Threshold of Maturity

Once that sweet connection with God that we had in the past feels missing or lacking, we just want it back so badly. God continually reminds us of our initial hunger. He teaches us lessons in the testing circumstances. Our desire grows to the point where the fear of obeying is less painful than the loss of God's felt Presence. The Shulamite looks for her lover but can't find him. Where is he? He's skipping on the mountains, of course. So, if she wants to see Him, she needs to be willing to go to the mountains.

A shift takes place when you realize that you want HIM more than you want anything else. Your hunger increases to get the intimacy back, and your heart cry is for Him and not for what He can do for you. It's the difference between seeking His face and not His hand: that is His Presence and not what He can do for you.

When your heart is ready to connect again at that deep level, ask yourself: What was that thing He asked me to do that I didn't do? What area is my spirit feeling conviction?

There are many other reasons that you may feel a distance from God and in *Appendix A Dialogue Journaling Tips* there are diagnostic questions to ask yourself to find your barriers. Confessing and repenting removes the static so you can clearly hear and see Him again. He moves you to the place where you can say yes to whatever He calls you to do. Obedience leads to a greater connection and increased glory and anointing.

One thing that every powerful fruit-bearing person in the Bible, in church history and the present day had is common is they said yes to God, no matter how scary the calling. This is what the Lord said about this threshold.

Fear is removed when a person understands that I AM. When I am with you, there is nothing to fear. My anointing power is with you when you align with My will. When I am directing your path, you will know the way. You are never alone because I AM. When I give you something to accomplish, I bring My full self to the job and fully equip you to carry it out.

It's all about understanding who I AM. I have heard people say..." God does not give you anything bigger than you can handle." This is not from Me. Of course, My plans are too big for you to handle! If it were easy, you would think you don't need Me. My plans are always BIG, and they are always GOOD. If you know those things about Me are true in your heart, then you come along side Me no matter how scary, crazy, big, or out there is MY calling!

You see, the secret to being able to accomplish your calling is to know who I AM. I can be trusted. So, trust Me. I created you uniquely for such a time as this to become who I already see you as; the real you, the Christ you, your Christ identity. Your Christ Identity is empowered completely by Me. I trust you for the job I've called you to do. Will you trust Me?

Start by obeying every heart prompt I give you, even the small ones. You will see that I am there to work through you. It's never you alone, and it's never Me alone. It's Me working through you as partners. Once you trust Me to see these truths in the small things, you will be able to trust Me to help you with the big stuff. Will you partner with Me for the plan I have for you?

Passing the Comfort Zone Test

In Song of Solomon Chapter 5, we see the shift in the Shulamite's heart, where she starts to seek her beloved earnestly. She asks people in the village if they have seen him. They tell her to look for his sheep. Sheep follow their Shepherd.

> John 10:27 (AMP) My sheep hear My voice, and I know them, and they follow Me;
>
> Song of Solomon 5:2 (AMP) I was asleep, but my heart was awake. A voice! My beloved was knocking: 'Open to me, my sister, my darling, My dove, my perfect one! For my head is drenched with dew, My locks with the damp of the night.'

She opened that door!

> Revelation 3:20 (AMP) [20] Behold, I stand at the door [of the church] and continually knock. If anyone hears My voice and opens the door, I will come in and eat with him (restore him), and he with Me.

The Bridegroom continually knocks and patiently calls you for higher purposes. When you pass the second test, a shift takes place in your heart, crossing you over the threshold to a clearer identity in Christ. Your thoughts and actions become more of a partnership with God. You trust God completely, unconditionally loving Him back.

Once you have crossed the threshold, committing to obeying Him without condition, something miraculous happens. God starts to release more power through you. You learn to trust Him entirely and become His partner. Suddenly, that book, mission trip, or new career holds excitement and not fear. Your heart has shifted to what you can do with God and not what He can do *for* you or what you can ever do *for* Him. Your heart loves Him and knows that He will be there to equip you for your calling.

Only weeks before Peter led 5,000 to Christ after receiving the Holy Spirit, he had denied Him three times. But now he was boldly speaking for Christ. The same thing that got Jesus crucified and had Peter too afraid to associate with Him only 50 days before was of no concern or barrier that day! That's what it looks like to cross the threshold. Your calling has come into focus. God begins to open doors. You begin to speak and act according to God's will. Miracles become common occurrences because **God trusts you** with increasing giftings. Because you have learned to trust Him, you become His trustworthy partner.

In the first four chapters, the Shulamite is concerned about her vineyard. There is a radical shift in her heart, and her vineyard becomes *his* vineyard. She has given him her whole heart.

You commit to give your heart to your spouse on your wedding day. You live life together, sharing everything with that person. You become ONE, united for all eternity. If people realized the level of spiritual significance that was happening on their wedding day, I believe we would have less divorce. Marriages founded on what your spouse can be and do **for** you rarely make it. Marriages that last have couples who partner, love, and serve each-other unconditionally.

Be the Bride

Who exactly is the Bride? Is it all believers in heaven? Or is it only those who have crossed the threshold and proven themselves to have been made ready? I believe that everyone who accepts the gift of salvation will be at the Wedding Feast of the Lamb. But will every believer in heaven be the Bride? In Matthew 22:1-22, Jesus tells the parable of the king who gave the wedding feast for his son. Many were invited to the celebration, but people were saying no. There were too many foxes, too many other priorities kept them from accepting this invitation. So, the king sent his servants out to find the people who were willing to come to the feast. Those who were willing to say yes filled the wedding hall.

> Revelation 3:21-22 The Passion Translation (TPT)²¹ And to the one who conquers[a] I will give the privilege of sitting with Me on my throne, just as I conquered and sat down with my Father on His throne.²² The one whose heart is open let him listen carefully to what the Spirit is saying now to the churches.

The verse says, "to the one who conquers." The Bible word for conquer is *nikaó* which means I conquer, am victorious, overcome, prevail, subdue.[15] Conquering sounds to me like passing the comfort zone test. I believe all born-again Christians will be at the Wedding Feast of the Lamb in heaven at the end of time. But those who cross that threshold will be the Bride that God trusts with the big jobs in heaven.

> Revelation 19:7-8 (AMP)⁷ Let us rejoice and be glad and give the glory to Him, for the marriage of the Lamb has come, and His[b] **bride has made herself ready**." ⁸ It was given to her to clothe herself in fine linen, bright and clean; for the fine linen **is the righteous acts of the**[c] **saints.**

To make yourself ready sounds like a condition to me. And righteous acts sound like the fruit-bearing of a calling. This is what trust and partnership look like. What does that feel like?

---

15   https://biblehub.com/greek/3528.htm Biblehub search term 'conquer'

John 16:33 (AMP) I have told you these things, so that in
Me you may have [perfect] peace. In the world, you have
tribulation and distress and suffering, but be courageous
[be confident, be undaunted, be filled with joy]; I have
overcome the world." [My conquest is accomplished, My
victory abiding.]

About the bride's partnership with Jesus, Mike Bickle summarizes:
"She walks out her mature bridal relationship with Jesus, which is
expressed in obedience (Song of Solomon 7:9-10). She expresses
bridal partnership in her intercession for more power (Song of
Solomon 7:11-13). She expresses her partnership in her boldness
of public ministry (Song of Solomon 8:1-2). She expresses her bridal
partnership in their full union (Song of Solomon 8:3-4)" [2]

It is the Bride that will co-reign with Jesus for eternity. Based on
this research, it is clear to me that not all of those with a ticket to
heaven are the Bride. Some will be guests at the Wedding Feast of the
Lamb, and some will be the Bride. Which will you be?

My Second Bridegroom Experience

I met the Bridegroom for the second time in Orlando at the Jesus 18'
event sponsored by *Jesus Image*. Michael Koulianis was facilitating
the last impartation experience before participants would leave
the three-day event. He was praying a "sending out with increased
anointing" impartation over the participants.

Michael recited verses from the Song of Solomon about the
Bride of Christ being made ready for the Bridegroom. He invited the
participants to go to the bridal chamber with Jesus. It was a call for
deeper intimacy.

I saw myself as a child dancing with Jesus, my feet on His feet, with Him swinging me around smiling. Dancing with Jesus is an experience I had had many times before. But when Michael suggested that we go into the bridal chamber, Jesus picked me up and put me on His shoulders and walked me into a room that had what looked like a hot tub filled with oil mixed with pure gold.

Jesus put me down and held my hand, and we walked into this pool and sat as you do in a hot tub where the water comes up to your chest, only we were sitting in gold-laced oil. We lifted our arms watching the dripping oil glisten with gold. I was weeping. The Bridegroom took my face with his oily hands and wiped a tear from my face. I noticed that He had a tear on His face, and that wrecked me even more. I wiped His tear with my oily thumb.

Then I heard Michael Koulianis increase the tempo of the music and intensity of his voice crying out for "MORE , MORE, MORE anointing." When he did this, Jesus stood up in the small pool and stretched out His arms. As He did so, He grew larger and larger. The pool grew as He did until as far as the eye can see there was oil and gold. As He rose, He transformed into the pure white, fire-eyed Jesus He is in the throne room witnessed by Ezekiel, Daniel, and John.

> Ezekiel 1:26-28 (AMP) [26] Now above the expanse that was over their heads there was something resembling a throne, it appeared like [it was made of] sapphire *or* lapis lazuli; and [seated] on that which looked like a throne, high up, was a figure with the appearance of a man. [27] Now upward, from that which appeared to be His waist, I saw something like glowing metal that looked like it was filled with fire all around it; and downward, from that which appeared to be His waist, I saw something like fire; and *there was* a brightness *and* a remarkable radiance [like a halo] around

126

Him. [28] As the appearance of the rainbow in the clouds on a rainy day, so was the appearance of the surrounding radiance. This was the appearance of the likeness of the glory *and* brilliance of the LORD. And when I saw it, I fell face downward and I heard a voice of One speaking.

Daniel 10:6 (AMP) His body was like beryl, his face like the brilliance of lightning, his eyes like flaming torches, his arms and legs like the gleam of polished bronze, and the sound of his words like the sound of a multitude.

John 1:12-16 (AMP) [12]Then I turned to see the voice that was speaking with me. And having turned, I saw seven golden lampstands, [13]and among the lampstands was One like the Son of Man, dressed in a long robe, with a golden sash around His chest. [14]The hair of His head was white like wool, as white as snow, and His eyes were like a blazing fire. [15]His feet were like polished bronze refined in a furnace, and His voice was like the roar of many waters. [16] He held in His right hand seven stars, and a sharp double-edged sword came from His mouth. His face was like the sun shining at its brightest.

It was so powerful; I can't even do justice describing it. He was showing me that together, we will accomplish much because of my partnership with Him. The gold represented the authority I have as His Bride. The oil symbolized the anointing power I have as His life partner.

At that same conference, Jess Koulianos taught about the Bridegroom. She challenged the audience to not casually date the Lord. That is when you seek God primarily when you want something; considering Him as being there only to meet your needs. But to be the Bride is a commitment to lifelong faithfulness! I'll never forget Jess saying, "Be the Bride that God can Trust. Have no other lovers!" It was one of the key take-aways I got from that conference.

Encountering the Bridegroom

A *Marriage Glimpse* – https://bit.ly/3iyTlcO

Steps for this encounter

- Spend some time in praise and worship before this encounter. Welcome God's Presence and ask Him to meet you in the Special Place.

- Meet Jesus in the Special Place as a child.

- Ask Jesus: Lord, show me where I am in my journey to Christian maturity... my level of trust and partnership and record what He says...

- Then ask Him: give me a glimpse of our marriage future whereby we are living a life together of trust and partnership... show me what I am like in this future and what kinds of things we are doing together to reflect you to the world.

Misty Edwards: "*I knew what I was getting into when I called you*" [3] – https://bit.ly/2DFoBbs

  - This is how the Lord feels about you when you say, YES!

  - Get in a quiet place and close your eyes and simply receive this love letter from the Lord.

  - Allow Him to meet you through the words of this song and then write down what you experienced.

Do this again... with the following differences...

  - The above link is a lyric video, so the second time you do it, you may want to see the words on the screen and write down some of the keywords that pierce your heart.

○   Then, go to the special place and thank the Lord for those specific things that He said that moved you!

Overcoming my Greatest Obstacles

- Meet Jesus in your special place as a child

- Spend a few minutes just having fun with Him

- Then ask Him: Lord, show me or talk with me about my greatest obstacles to my spiritual growth. What is one step I can take today to overcome them?

- Then thank Him and purpose in your spirit to take that step.

[1] https://lancewallnau.com/category/7-mountains/

[2] An Overview of the Storyline in the Song of Solomon by Mike Bickle, video recording 02/2014 https://mikebickle.org/watch/2014_02_14_1800_FCF_MB

[3] This is a portion of a live musical oracle (that is a musical download message from the Lord) given to Misty Edwards from the International House of Prayer in Kansas City many years ago. The original oracle was 21 minutes long. This is 9 minutes, my favorite version of it. It was inspired by Song of Solomon Chapter 8, where the Bride has reached her spiritual maturity and reveals how it moves the heart of God to see her this way!

[i] "The Song of Songs" "Studies in the Song of Solomon: Progression of Holy Passion" (2007) Book Author: Mike Bickle

https://archive.org/details/SongOfSongs_CompleteSet/SongOfSongs04.mp3

I Will be Your Friend by Michael W Smith

https://bit.ly/3gUsZ4s

Meet the Friend

❧

Reflect on your entire life for a moment. Think about the people in your life who are or have been your dearest friends. Seasons of friends come and go, but true friendship has certain commonalities. Close friends are people you enjoy, have fun with, laugh, and spend time. More importantly, you share your heart with them in the most difficult of times.

The Lord is the perfect Friend to us. The word friend in the Bible is *phílos*.[16] It means someone dearly loved, prized in a personal and intimate way, a trusted confidant, or held dear and close in a bond of personal affection. The Lord adds the perfection of *agapáō*[17] to His friendship with us, the unconditional and perfect love of God's Omni-benevolence. The Fruit of the Spirit reveals and defines this kind of love for us.

> Galatians 5:22-23 (AMP) [22] But the fruit of the Spirit [the result of His Presence within us] is love [unselfish concern for others], joy, [inner] peace, patience [not the ability to wait, but how we act while waiting], kindness, goodness,

---

16 https://biblehub.com/greek/5384.htm Biblehub search word "friend"
17 https://biblehub.com/str/greek/25.htm Biblehub search word "love"

faithfulness, [23] gentleness, self-control. Against such things there is no law.

Don't those verses describe the kind of friend you would want to have in your life? Joy is the aspect of the fruit that is emphasized in the Name "Friend." Notice that joy is the first defining characteristic of the Love of God. Since there were no other ways to indicate emphasis for Bible writers, they ordered things to show importance. If we are not living a life of love, joy, and peace, we miss God's best. God is the absolute best friend you can ever have. He is by His very nature, your Friend. The bigger question is, are you His friend?

Friendship in the Proverbs

King Solomon was considered the wisest man who ever lived. He wrote the book of Proverbs. Here is just some of what the Lord gave Him to say about friendship:

> Proverbs 18:24, NLT There are "friends" who destroy each other, but a real friend sticks closer than a brother.
>
> Proverbs 27:5-6, NLT An open rebuke is better than hidden love! Wounds from a sincere friend are better than many kisses from an enemy.
>
> Proverbs 17:17, NLT A friend is always loyal, and a brother is born to help in time of need.
>
> Proverbs 27:9, NLT The heartfelt counsel of a friend is as sweet as perfume and incense.
>
> Proverbs 27:17, NLT As iron sharpens iron, so a friend sharpens a friend.

From these verses, we learn that friends love and challenge you to be a better person. Here the Lord is challenging you to ask honestly;

are you allowing the Lord to be your Friend? Are you getting close enough to allow Him to speak into your life? Do you respect His instruction and know it is motivated by perfect love so that it may transform you?

God's Friends in the Bible

Moses was God's friend. At that time, Moses was unique in this way. Speaking face to face is God's heart's desire for all of His people.

> Exodus 33:11 (AMP) [11]"And so the Lord used to speak to Moses' face to face, just as a man speaks to his friend."

> Abraham was God's friend.

> James 2:23 (AMP) [23] "And the Scripture was fulfilled which says, "Abraham believed God, and this [faith] was credited to him [by God] as righteousness and as conformity to His will," and he was called the friend of God."

Abraham believed God's promises were true and real, no matter what He asked him to do. In Abraham, we learn that faith is not only a factor in friendship but the fruit of it. Jesus' faithful followers were and are His friends.

> John 15:13-15 (AMP) [13]" No one has greater love [nor stronger commitment] than to lay down his own life for his friends. [14] You are my friends if you keep on doing what I command you. [15] I do not call you servants any longer, for the servant does not know what his master is doing; but I have called you [My] friends, because I have revealed to you everything that I have heard from My Father."

Jesus is showing here that laying down His life was a demonstration of His friendship's depth. Many have made the same sacrifice for Him.

Obedience is a measure of your relationship. Jesus has given you the Holy Spirit to guide you into all righteousness. He has given you the capability to obey by sharing God's will. He shows you the way day-by-day to align your life accordingly.

Because you have the indwelling Holy Spirit, this opportunity exists for you to know His friendship and to demonstrate yours. The encounters that you have with the Names of God facilitate and increase your friendship with Him.

Likeability

We have already established that God loves everyone. He can't not love you. It's who He is, not what He feels. It's His "IS-NESS," His core identity, and the motivation behind everything He does. But liking is a different story. The book *Influence* by Robert Cialdini [1] identifies six human nature motivations.

These influencers affect everyone and can be used for good by blessing people, or evil as manipulations. Cialdini asserts that:

- We will do things for people that we like that we would not do for people that we don't like.

- You tend to like people who like you.

- You like people that make you feel safe.

- You like people that make you feel comfortable and welcome.

- You like people that you sense as trustworthy.

These are common sense factors. Looking at these statements from your perspective as you think of those for whom you like, it's easy to see. Now flip the perspective for a moment. Could the Lord say you are His friend based upon these factors? Do you make Him feel welcome? Have you proven yourself trustworthy to obey His voice? Can He count you as someone for whom He enjoys quality time spent?

The Favor Anointing

Favor is an anointing force. The word favorite comes from the word favor. *Charin*[18] is the word for favor in the Bible. It means; yearn towards, long for, be merciful, compassionate, favorable, inclined towards, give, grant graciously. Lance Wallnau calls it the *honey of heaven* because it is sticky and sweet. It's when you dip yourself in God's blessed Presence, and He sticks to you in a way that people can sense. He defines favor as "the attraction of God to you that releases an influence through you so that other people are included to like, trust and cooperate with you in an assignment God gave you connected to your calling."

Favor is a magnetic force that God puts on you because you have befriended Him. Remembering that the word anointing is *chrió*[19], It is a material substance of the very presence of God on you. It literally means to rub or smear and to consecrate for a purpose. Based on that definition, it makes sense that you must be in His Presence to receive it.

What Jesus said about the Anointing

This was a journal discussion I had with the Lord about the anointing.

---

18 https://biblehub.com/greek/5485.htm Biblehub search word "favor"
19 https://biblehub.com/greek/5485.htm Biblehub search word "to anoint"

Lord, I never really thought about the anointing as rubbing off of YOU on things and people. It was fascinating to learn that the anointing is a material substance. Please help me understand this rubbing/smearing. Help me see it with the eyes of my heart what you want me to know about it.

God reminded me of when my prayer partner Becky poured gallons of oil on a lady at the Cleveland House of Prayer. I was experiencing the Misty Edwards Bridegroom encounter for the first time. Then the Lord showed me an imprint like a stamp, wet at first, and then dried in place as a permanent tattoo, marked and sealed.

> *The more boldly you wear Me for all to see, the more rubbing of the anointing will dry permanently like a tattoo. People will feel Me when they are near you. They will know Me because of your boldness. Elijah's bones were so saturated with My Presence that every atom and neuron was drenched with my anointing and remained on the prophet's bones because of his boldness for Me. It was a permanent imprint.*

> *Memory foam receives an imprint and then pops back after you take your hands off it. But when it happens repeatedly an imprint remains. Evidence of it lingers visible even after a person gets up. The same is true when the anointing is present continually in your life.*

Bible Stories of the Favor Anointing

Nehemiah

Nehemiah was the cupbearer of King Artaxerxes at the tail end of Israel's 70-year exile. Word got back to Nehemiah that the city walls of Jerusalem were in shambles, and it weighed heavily on his heart.

One day, the king noticed a solemnness in Nehemiah and asked him what was wrong. Feeling his pain, the king asked Nehemiah how he could help.

> Nehemiah 2:7-9 (AMP) [7] Then I said to the king, "If it pleases the king, let letters be given to me for the governors of the provinces beyond the [Euphrates] River, so that they will allow me to pass through until I reach Judah, [8] and a letter to Asaph, the keeper of the king's forest, so that he will give me timber to construct beams for the gates of the fortress which is by the temple, and for the city wall and for the house which I will occupy." **And the king granted me what I asked, for the good hand of my God was upon me.**
>
> [9] Then I came to the governors of the provinces beyond the [Euphrates] River and gave them the king's letters. **Now the king had sent officers of the army and horsemen with me.**

The Cupbearer's job was to taste and test the food and drink before the king. Poisoning was a common way to kill kings in that day. Because of Nehemiah's trusting relationship, the king granted him everything he needed to go and repair the walls of Jerusalem.

When Nehemiah arrived in Jerusalem, each family situated closest to the sections of the wall stepped up and repaired their wall portion under Nehemiah's anointed instruction. Remarkably, they completed the job in only fifty two days! The king and the people who helped did so because of the favor anointing on Nehemiah.

Moses and the Israelites

After so many plagues hitting the people of Egypt, you would have expected the Egyptians to hate the Israelites. In Pharaoh's stubbornness, the people experience plague after plague, even costing them their firstborn. The Lord forecasted the favor for the Israelites even before the plagues affected them.

> Exodus 3:21- 22 (AMP) [21] And I will grant this people favor and respect in the sight of the Egyptians; therefore, it shall be that when you go, you will not go empty-handed. [22] But every woman shall [insistently] ask her neighbor and any woman who [a]lives in her house, for articles of silver and articles of gold, and clothing; and you shall put them on your sons and daughters. In this way you are to plunder the Egyptians [leaving bondage with great possessions that are rightfully yours]."

Why did God give more than 2 tons of silver, gold, linens, and other treasures to more than 2 million people exiting Egypt? Because they would need them to build the temple to serve the Lord. The favor anointing is always connected to Kingdom purposes.

Mary, Joseph, and baby Jesus

Joseph and Mary were from a modest family. They did not have a lot of money. When Jesus was an infant, they were told by an angel to go to Egypt:

> Matthew 2:13-14 (AMP) [13] Now when they had gone, an angel of the Lord appeared to Joseph in a dream and said, "Get up! Take the Child and His mother and flee to Egypt and remain there until I tell you; for Herod intends to search for the child to destroy Him." [14] So Joseph got up and took the Child and His mother while it was still night and left for Egypt. [15] He remained there until the death of Herod. This was to fulfill what the Lord had spoken by the prophet [Hosea]: "Out of Egypt I called My Son."

138

It was Mary and Joseph's purpose and calling to raise the Messiah. And this action fulfilled a prophetic promise from hundreds of years before. There was special favor over the ones the Father would trust for that job! So He made sure they were provided for and put a burning purpose on some Magi hearts from a distant land to provide for them.

> Matthew 2:9-11 (AMP) [9] After hearing the king, they went their way; and behold, the star, which they had seen in the east, went on before them [continually leading the way] until it came and stood over the place where the young child was. [10] When they saw the star, they rejoiced exceedingly with great joy. [11] And after entering the house, they saw the Child with Mary, His mother; and they fell down and worshiped Him. Then, after opening their treasure chests, **they presented to Him gifts [fit for a king, gifts] of gold, frankincense, and myrrh.**

Jesus was about two years old when the magi presented these gifts. The star appeared on the night He was born, and God led these men for two years until they could give their gifts to the King of kings. God's magnetic influence can reach people across the world!

Two sides of the Favor Magnet

Magnets stick and repel. Likewise, there are two sides to the favor anointing. The enemy hates God's favor! Consequently, as God increases your favor and people magnetically show up to help you, prepare for spiritual warfare.

The favor anointing is like the supernatural radius of God's love that surrounds you and makes people notice and sense God's love, causing them to want to help you. The enemy uses jealousy as a mighty weapon against the power of the favor anointing. Have you noticed that many of the most fruit-bearing Spirit-led leaders experience their most significant resistance from **inside** the body of Christ? This is because jealousy can be an ugly enemy to the purposes of God.

To handle the power of the favor anointing, you must have the character of God reigning in your heart. Attacks will come. The challenge is to keep your eyes fixed on Jesus and not on the haters, understanding that spiritual warfare is typical, and knowing that the One in you is so much greater than the one in the world is necessary to keep in balance. Do not fear the favor anointing because of this truth; embrace it.

The more time you spend with Jesus, the more He will transform you into the person that can handle increasing spiritual warfare levels. Do not keep your eyes fixed on the warfare, or it will grow more prominent in your heart. Pray for those who are against you and continue to keep your heart aligned with the Lord. You will be able to handle it.

One super clear Bible story that shows the two sides of the favor magnet is the love-hate relationship between King Saul and David. After David was anointed as a future king, God's anointing left King Saul. This vacuum filled with tormenting spirits causing the king great anguish. Saul found comfort when David played the harp for him. The soothing presence of the Lord on David and the relaxing instrumental music of the harp gave King Saul peace. In David's presence, Saul loved him like a son.

But soon jealousy overtook King Saul as the people preferred David and taunted him with songs comparing David to Saul. This jealousy turned into murderous hatred, and he hunted David on a mission to kill him for many years. David had many opportunities to kill Saul but would not dare kill God's anointed King. This hunting season covered eight years and is thoroughly covered in 1 Samuel chapters 21-31 and 2 Samuel chapter 1.

At one point, David got close enough to cut off a fringe of Saul's robe and then confronted him about it. In David's presence, look what happens to Saul:

> 1 Samuel 24:16-19 (AMP) Then Saul wept aloud [17]and said to David, "You are more righteous than I, for you have rewarded me with good, though I have rewarded you with evil. [18]And you have shown this day how well you have dealt with me; for when the LORD delivered me into your hand, you did not kill me. [19]When a man finds his enemy, does he let him go away unharmed? May the LORD reward you with good for what you have done for me this day.

Saul winds up blessing David and leaving him alone until the next chapter when he is no longer in David's favor anointed presence and resumes the hunt!

How Friendship with God Develops

It is a great privilege to be counted as one of God's friends. It comes from spending time praising and worshiping Him for pure enjoyment. The more time you spend with the Lord in His Presence for no personal agenda other than to Be with Him, the more His Presence rubs off on you. People can sense it and are attracted to it. It is as simple as that. Enjoy Him. Be the friend to God that you would have always wanted.

Jesus is just like us in friendship. He likes people who like Him, trust Him, make Him feel welcome, and those for whom He can count on to obey Him. When you gaze at Jesus, He gazes back at you. Where His eyes are fixed, His favor and transformational power flow. If you prioritize Him, He prioritizes you!

A properly postured heart is the key to befriending Jesus. Spending time praising and worshiping Him, meditating on the Bible with Him, singing, and praying in tongues let Him know that You prioritize Him. Meet Him without agendas. Just enjoy His presence! These are all ways to make Jesus feel welcome, prioritized, and trusted. These face-to-face actions show God that you are His friend.

God Knows His Friends Before they are His Friends

God is omniscient. He lives outside of time and space. He knows every decision you will ever make, not because He's a puppet master causing you to make them. His omniscient vantage point has seen you make them already. There are times when you may not even realize that He was trying to show you something about your future levels of favor long before you earned them by your devotion.

Mary was a young teenager, probably 14 years old when the Angel Gabriel approached her and told her she would be the highly favored mother of the Messiah. David was a teenage shepherd boy whose father did not even count him worthy of being included when Samuel showed up to anoint one of his sons as the next king. We just don't see it in ourselves, and doubtless others around us don't see it either yet.

I have told the following story probably more than a dozen times in my life. Yet, it was only in preparation for this chapter that the Lord gave me additional insight about it.

One year after graduating from college (only a short 2 ½ years after my salvation), I was driving on the highway to Columbus to meet my former college roommates for a brief reunion. I was in the passing lane. There was a guardrail to my left, another lady driving a car to my right, and the Barnum and Bailey Circus parked on the berm for what felt like a few miles.

Coming toward me full speed was a white car. Time slowed down for me, and what was probably only a few seconds seemed to last for several minutes. During the slow-motion time, I talked to Jesus, reflecting on the impending consequence of my present reality. I had an unreasonable amount of peace in my heart as I thanked the Lord that I knew Him and that I would be with Him in heaven in a few moments. I reminded the Lord that it would have been nice to have the opportunity to get married and have children. Then I reminded myself that the Lord is the one who grants us our days. I was honestly OK with it.

I looked to the right and thought how odd it was that the circus was there. I looked into the eyes of the lady driving next to me, and her eyes seemed to ask: "Are you going to take me with you?" I gave her an assuring look that said, "No, I won't swing into your lane."

As the white car was directly in front of me, I noticed out of the corner of my eye that the guardrail had disappeared. I immediately turned my wheel to the left and looked into the driver's eyes and had two thoughts. First was: "Oh no... Now I'm probably going to be maimed or paralyzed for the rest of my life when I could have been with Jesus." And, I noticed how vacant and dead the man's eyes looked. I felt sad.

Instantly, I felt an earthquake-like shaking of the car from the wind of this man's car passing mine. He did not hit me, and there was not a scratch on me or the car. I found myself in the dip of the median strip between the highways. Suddenly, time sped back to normal, and then it hit me how close I was to getting killed. I started shaking and crying uncontrollably.

A man from the circus crossed the highway to check on me. He said he honestly thought he was about to witness the worst crash of his life and was glad that I was OK. He offered to help me, and I said I would be fine. I just needed time to stop shaking. He assured me that he had notified the Highway Patrol with his CB radio.

When I finally got to my destination, the circus man was telling the story to a news reporter on TV. I learned that the white car driver had run three more people off the road before the Highway Patrol stopped him. No one was injured. His wife had just died, and he was suicidal and didn't care who he took with him. The circus was on the berm because some elephants were vomiting, and they needed to stop the caravan and attend to them. These animals were used to traveling, so this was unusual.

As many times as I have told that story, the Lord unveiled some nuggets that I had never really noticed before. There were multiple miracles; many things had lined up perfectly for this story to happen. God slowed down time for me to reflect on my life. The Lord caused elephants to vomit so the circus would stop on the side of the road and prevent anyone from getting off the highway at the exact time I would be driving. That woman was driving next to me at the same moment to prevent me from moving into her lane. No doubt the Lord was speaking to her too! The guardrail disappeared, and I was able to turn the wheel in the exact time to stay safe. The distraught man was recklessly endangering people. Yet, the Lord protected him and did not allow anyone to be injured on his mission. I had a conversation with the Lord that I was not spiritually mature enough to have at that time in my stage of faith. The Lord Himself gave me those thoughts.

But the most crucial lesson of it was that the Lord orchestrated all of that to show me that He had big plans for me. It was not my time to go to heaven. Even the saving of me in that time of my life was His favor connected to my future calling. He was forecasting that He had a good reason to keep me alive!

Have you ever had a close call? Was there a time that you could have died but you didn't? Perhaps God was telling you that He had big plans for you, and He just wanted you to know that it wasn't your time.

Favor Can be Lost

The quickest way to lose God's favor is to take pride in His blessings. Your character must be rock solid to handle the force of favor. You must be able to recognize God's hand in your blessings. Everything is a test. When good things happen, thank the Lord for them.

Another way you can lose God's favor is to allow the spiritual warfare to become more prominent in your mind than God. If you let what people say and do crush you, you give the enemy more power than is deserved. You make the enemy bigger in your mind and heart than God, which is a slippery slope.

Finally, favor can be lost if you stop prioritizing your time with God. If you received favor because you spend time with God and then allow busyness to back burner Him, you will lose His favor. Creating holy habits of abiding with Him will continually strengthen your character, keep your eyes fixed on Jesus, and keep the favor flowing.

The Secret Power of Joy

The Lord revealed a secret to me about keeping that bigger spiritual tank filled up with ease. Psalm 16:11 shows you the secret.

> Psalm 16:11 (AMP) [11] You will show me the path of life; In Your presence **is fullness of joy**;
> In Your right hand there are pleasures forevermore.

You can see from this verse that there is a connection with finding the path of life and God's Presence and fullness of joy. Fullness is an absolute word. It is *pléróma*[20] in the Bible, which means complete satisfaction, fulfillment, completion.

To help me understand this, the Lord reminded me of the movie *Monster's Inc.*[21] This is an animated film for children about a monster world that gets the energy to power their city with the fear and screams of children. Monsters enter the children's bedrooms through closet doors at night and scare them to produce electricity that is captured to power their monster city.

The movie follows Sully and Mike, a monster scaring team competing for the best scare record in the company against archrival villain Randall. A small child who they named Boo accidentally crosses into the monster world. Children are assumed to be toxic, and they need to get her back home as quickly as possible. The film's villain, Randall pursues this child throughout this film.

---

20 https://biblehub.com/greek/4138.htm Biblehub search word "fullness"
21 https://youtu.be/-2fmN4E0DK0 YouTube search "Monsters Inc Boo laughs

Most of the time, this toddler has no idea she is in danger, and she feels safe with Sully and Mike. There is a critical shift in the film when Mike makes Boo laugh. Her laughter causes the power grid to go so high that it powers the entire city for a few seconds, and nearly blows the power circuits! Here is a short clip from the movie:

https://youtu.be/-2fmN4E0DK0

The fear and scream energy are like running on the enemy's fuel. When you listen to the enemy's voice and agree with his negativity, it is like you are running your car on harmful gas. Over time, this will kill your engine and break the car. Likewise, focusing too much on negative energy robs you of physical vibrancy, emotional, mental, and spiritual health. This is what the Lord had to say about this movie's message:

In the Monster's Inc. movie, you see the power contrast between fear and joy. As you move along the spiritual maturity continuum toward your purpose and calling, there is a need for increased levels of anointing.

With an increase of anointing, your heart container must enlarge to handle this new level. When you have crossed over the threshold and become the Bride, you are in My friendzone.

I am always your Friend, but here, you become My friend. This is because your heart has shifted from seeing Me as a genie whose purpose is to meet your wants and needs to a God worthy of your time, praise and worship. You have prioritized time with Me just for Me. Holy habits of seeking My face and not My hand begin to take hold and are critical at this phase of your journey.

This newfound relationship with Me expands your heart's ability to handle increased levels of My anointing power. I know your needs, so you don't need to come to Me as a beggar. You are the daughter or son of the King of kings. I already know your needs. Here is a secret to quickly filling up your heart tank: joy is a booster! It's a thousand-fold multiplier. In My presence, there is FULLNESS of JOY! (See Psalm 16:11)

We learned in the Monsters Inc. movie that one heartfelt giggle from a child could power the entire city! There is supernatural anointing energy from Me that comes from you enjoying Me for Me.

The same amount of time in My presence will have different levels of anointing energy. Seeking my hand that is asking for what I can do for you has some benefit. But MUCH greater is the same amount of time spent with Me with a heart of gratitude and joy. Thanking me even for trials brings increased levels of my anointing power and favor.

Just have childlike fun with Me, and the favor anointing flows as high-quality supernatural gas for your tank! Bigger tanks need more fuel. Joy is the secret to filling up your bigger tank with the best stuff in a short amount of time.

Encountering the Friend

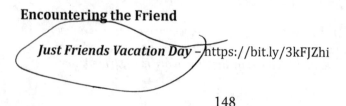

***Just Friends Vacation Day –** https://bit.ly/3kFJZhi*

Steps for this encounter

- Pack your spiritual bags. You and your Friend Jesus are going on vacation. This is a supernatural vacation encounter, so expect it to defy the laws of nature!
- Spend some time in praise and worship before this encounter. Plan for this one to take between 8 and 10 minutes, even though the recording will be very short.
- Meet Jesus in your special place as a child with your packed suitcase.
- Allow Him to take you on a vacation that He only knows your heart desires. Do something with Him that you always wanted to do... Want to travel to a part of the world? Want to skydive? Enjoy snow skiing? Go to the moon? Do it with Jesus.

- Laugh, wonder, enjoy it together! He knows where He wants you to go and what you would want to do!

Bible Story - The Wedding in Cana – https://bit.ly/300DrF4

Steps for this encounter

- Meet Jesus in your special place.

- Let Jesus take you to the Wedding in Cana as His plus one!

- Read and meditate on the verses about the Wedding in Cana

Miracle at Cana

> John 2: 1-11 (AMP) On the third day there was a wedding at Cana of Galilee, and the mother of Jesus was there; [2] and both Jesus and His disciples were invited to the wedding.
>
> [3] When the wine was all gone, the mother of Jesus said to Him, "[a]They have no *more* wine." [4] Jesus said to her, "[Dear] woman, [b]what is that to you and to Me? My time [to act and to be revealed] has not yet come."

[5] His mother said to the servants, "Whatever He says to you, do it."

[6] Now there were six stone water pots set there for the Jewish custom of purification (ceremonial washing), containing twenty or thirty gallons each.

[7] Jesus said to the servants, "Fill the water pots with water." So they filled them up to the brim.

[8] Then He said to them, "Draw *some* out now and take it to the headwaiter [of the banquet]." So they took it *to him*.

[9] And when the headwaiter tasted the water which had turned into wine, not knowing where it came from (though the servants who had drawn the water knew) he called the bridegroom,

[10] and said to him, "Everyone else serves his best wine first, and when *people* have [c]drunk freely, *then he serves* that which is not so good; but you have kept back the good wine until now."

[11] This, the first of His signs (attesting miracles), Jesus did in Cana of Galilee, and revealed His glory [displaying His deity and His great power openly], and His disciples believed [confidently] in Him [as the Messiah—they adhered to, trusted in, and relied on Him].

- Enjoy this wedding celebration with Him... dance, sing, meeting some disciples, congratulate the Bride and Groom, meet His mother, Mary...

- Watch His first miracle!

Do it again: Just Friends or a Bible Story encounter with different activities and different Bible stories. Ask the Lord what He would want to do with you. Simply meet Him and let Him take you where He wants.

[1] *Influence: How and Why People Agree to Things,* by Robert Cialdini, Ph.D., Copywrite 1984 by Robert Cialdini, Quill, NY, NY

[2] https://www.kenblanchardbooks.com/

Somehow You Want Me by Tenth Avenue North

https://bit.ly/3fSJ1L5

LOVE Book Conclusion

〰️

*I*t wasn't the first time the Lord took me on a magic carpet ride. Each time is wonderful! I always learn something amazing on each trip. This time, we flew around the whole world. Jesus wanted to show me His heart for all the people groups who still needed to know Him. I saw faces of every race, age, and status and felt His compassionate yearning for them.

When the ride was nearly over, He flipped the carpet, so we were flying upside down lower to the ground. This was cooler than any amusement park ride! Surprisingly, I wasn't scared. There was no sensation of falling as I was stuck to the carpet with the wind blowing through my hair and a wild upside-down perspective of the world! Then Jesus talked to me about the object lesson of this experience.

I am your gravity. You are naturally and gently pulled to Me. There is no fear when you are with Me. People don't doubt gravity. They trust and believe in it without thought. They know that gravity is REAL.

The truth is that gravity doesn't require you to believe in it to BE true. It IS True. You are not a factor in the truth of gravity.

The same is true of Me. I AM whether people believe in Me or not. You did not speak creation into existence. That was My job.

It's weird that people trust gravity, and struggle with trusting Me, the Creator of gravity. It grieves Me that so many don't know how alive and present I am. I created people to connect with Me like you have taught them to do in this book. Some people will argue; "Patty is different, or special because she can hear God so personally, but I can't do that." That is a limiting lie. You are special to Me but you are simply showing people how to live out the Biblical truths that are available for every believer.

I created everyone to be able to connect with Me personally and the Word clearly shows the way. I am here for everyone in all ways. My heart longs for you. I came to give you abundant life. Connecting with Me individually is one of the secrets to growing your faith and trust to navigate this world. I want people to stop looking for Me in dusty attic boxes marked "religious stuff" when the truth is, I'm right HERE! I'm sitting in plain sight and waiting to LOVE each one in their special places.

Take the Red Pill- the Matrix Metaphor

Just about every theology or religion can claim some sort of connection with The Matrix movies. I don't want to get too deep into this allegory of spirituality, but the Lord pointed out so many interesting themes that reflect key points of this book.

The 1999 film is set in a dystopian earth where people think the world they live in is real, but their world is a computer game created by aliens who found a way to power their world by the electrical capabilities of human bodies. Only a small remnant learns how to find the truth.

The science fiction film even names their characters for spiritual realities. Morpheous, a name that makes me think of transformation is a Holy Spirit archetype. He finds, trains, and guides the prophesied one, Neo, who represents the Savior who would rescue the earth from the bondage of Agents. They represent the dark principalities of the enemy. The Oracle, like the Heavenly Father, represents the source of prophetic guidance and Truth. Trinity is the team member that loves our hero so much it leads to his resurrection from the dead.

The point of the film is that truth is more powerful than counterfeits. Real is not what you think it is. Just because it's normal, doesn't make it true. There is a truth that is right there that can set you free. You just need to choose this reality.

The Truth of God must be experienced to be understood. When we started this journey, we learned about God's TV channel. It's the alpha brainwave that helps us connect with the Omni God that dwells in the hearts of Christians. We learned about four keys that we can use to communicate with God using the eyes and ears of our hearts.

This is a cool film clip from the Matrix movie to illustrate these principles. Matrix Red/Blue pill scene

https://bit.ly/31ILu5L

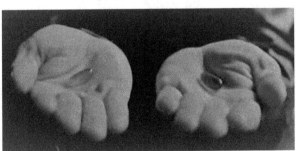

The spiritual realm is all around and within you. You chose to take the red pill when you picked up this book. You learned the truth that God is not a distant and unloving God that you can call on but can't hear you. He is right here within you. He's waiting to have adventures with you.

To connect with God completely, you needed to forget everything you thought you knew about Him and come to Him as a child. Taking the spiritual red pill, you realized just how close, intimate, and loving is your God. You learned how to stop praying distant genie-like prayers to a faraway God and connect with the pure heart and joy of the ever-present Omni God.

In another scene of the Matrix, while Neo was waiting to talk to Oracle, he sees a small child bending the spoon by simply looking at it. She hands him a spoon and says, "Don't try to bend the spoon. That's impossible. The truth is it's not the spoon that is bending it is yourself." The Lord is not limited in any way by the natural laws of this world. He created this world, but the real world, the eternal world is heaven. And we do not need to die to encounter heaven now.

In messianic fashion, Neo is killed by the agents and rises from the dead by the power of Trinity's faith. We learned that even the ability to have faith comes from God. The newly risen Neo realizes his identity and power and easily defeats the enemy. You can too! When you realize who you are in Christ, the capability of your Christ-Identity, you begin to live out your destiny with the power to conquer every challenge in your life.

The Names You Met and Key Lessons

Even before we met any specific names, we had our first encounter in the *Special Place* where we could build our memories with Jesus by each Name in a private and safe place. Here again are the Names you met and the key lessons learned and experienced by encountering them.

The Heavenly Father- The Power of Child-like Faith

When you met the **Heavenly Father,** you learned how to tap into God's TV channel by meeting Him as a child. The tender love of God is most received when you posture your heart with the faith of a child. Picturing yourself as a child is essential to the connection with the Lord in your heart. He is not a distant God but rather as close as breathing. Learning to tune to the indwelling Holy Spirit by connecting with Him in your special place as a child is the first step to increasing your love and trust in God. The Heavenly Father is the best starting point Name for the journey.

The alpha brain wave is a vehicle to connecting to the God TV channel. Even though your childhood and your parents were not perfect, God can show you how to see Him as a safe Father. The child you are in the Spirit, the real you, and is more playful and secure in His Presence than the child that you were when you were young. Allowing yourself to spend time with God the Father will open doors to Him in your heart you didn't even know were there.

The Heavenly Father took us back to our childhood in the Remember Me encounter and we played and found healing in the Missions Trip to the Inner Child and exchanged Love letters with Him.

The Savior- Surrender and Identity

When you met the **Savior,** He showed you the level of surrender that He was willing to give to the Father to redeem you from the slavery caused by Adam and Eve's first sin. He showed you the level of importance that communion with all people means to the LORD and how His sacrifice resolved the conflicting truths of God's justice, righteousness, mercy, love, and grace.

We looked at how the Father outdid Himself with an impressive and incalculable statistic of 353 fulfilled prophecies (and still counting) of showing that not only was Jesus the only One who could have ever been the Messiah but that He is alive and still working mightily today in the hearts of born-again Spirit-led believers. Come to think of it, let's make it 354 as the Revelation 12:1-4 sign in the heavens was predicted and then manifested and carefully recorded by astronomers on September 23, 2017![22]

We learned that even the faith to believe God comes from God and not from you. Trying or striving clicks off the God TV channel. Surrendering is the only way to connect to the Savior. We learned that your ticket to heaven can be cashed in right now and cannot be lost. You have an inheritance and authority to live out your salvation right now which includes healing, direction, and power.

You met Jesus inside the tomb and talked with Him about why He went through the crucifixion experience for you. He explained the Great Exchange and you experienced the Baptism of the Holy Spirit.

Immanuel: Abiding Lifestyle

The Name **Immanuel** highlights for you the Omni-Truth of God's Ever-Presence. When you accept the gift of Salvation, the Holy Spirit dwells in your heart with the fullness of His Nature, Character, and Power.

---

22 https://en.wikipedia.org/wiki/Revelation_12_sign_prophecy#/media/File:Revelation_12_Sign.gif

The more time you spend with Immanuel, the more sensitivity you have to His supernatural Presence. Living this naturally supernatural lifestyle is absent from striving. You discovered Christ lives in you and helps you with all areas of your life. He allows you to see the world through His eyes, hear through His ears, and connect with His mind, will, and emotion. When you abide in Christ, you come into alignment with His perfect will and begin to make His choices for you. Learning to live out of your Christ Identity one day at a time is the fruit of your relationship with Immanuel.

You experienced the spiritual truths of what in means to be IN Christ with the *In His Skin* and *Seeing His Covering* encounters with Immanuel. You also had Him talk to you about the practical skill of having Him *Order your Day*.

Bridegroom- Key Lessons: Trust and Partnership

As you know from life, there is a big difference between casually dating and the commitment of marriage. The same is true for understanding the **Bridegroom**. You learned about the journey to Christian maturity as you moved from trusting Him to meet our needs to becoming His devoted life partner as the Bride.

You grasped the challenges and tests that needed to be passed to move you along in your relationship with the Bridegroom through the lens of the Song of Solomon.

Your encounters gave you a *marriage glimpse* where you could see what it looked like for you to be living with God as a full partner. You experienced the joy the Bridegroom has for His bride in the *Misty Edwards* encounter base on the Song of Solomon chapter 8. The Bridegroom clarified for you some tips for overcoming your *greatest obstacles* to making a full commitment as the bride.

Friend- Key Lessons: Likeability, Joy, and the Favor Anointing.

You discovered that Jesus is the perfect **Friend** and what it would take for you to be considered His friend. You examined the force of the favor anointing and what it takes to manage its magnetic power. You found the secret power of joy and how just being with God and having fun fills up your spiritual tank on the maximum spigot.

We spent a full day with Jesus our Friend on a *supernatural vacation* doing things that we could only do with Him. We practiced jumping into a Bible story as we joined Jesus and His disciples as His guest at the *wedding in Cana.*

How Jesus showed up! Encounter Stories from Others

- **Missions Trip to the Inner Child encounter (Roma Flood)**

I climbed onto Jesus's knee and we had a chat. I asked Him; "what's the truth that will set me free?"

Believing in childlike faith is the key to freedom. Coming as a child allows you to come with no expectations or preconceived ideas. And with the simplicity to be excited about what I can say and do.

We can enjoy time together, exchanging words and laughter by simply enjoying being with one another. When you encounter the real Me of the gospel, you can come in childlike faith. This is how you truly know Me. When the knowledge of Me is misconstrued and tied up in past experiences and misinterpretations of the word, confusion and every evil work sets in and robs you of your joy and your gifts and the promises that belong to you. When you know the Truth you know Me and you are free. Simply free to be you.

Oh gosh Lord, I've been so left brained that I haven't allowed you into my world. I strive to learn more and do more for you; to attain perfection or know more. But I could not ever get there. Now I know and believe it's so simple. I have experienced it today for myself. Thank you, Jesus!

- **Resurrection Encounter (George Medellin)**

I am sitting with Jesus inside the tomb and ask: "why did you go through this?"

Because before the foundation of the world, son, I loved you and the world. As much as I love you, I thought of and bled for every person ever born on the earth. Those fully born, those dying at birth, those dying before birth, and those dying from horrific childhoods. Oh, son! I love each person as a father loves his own son or daughter. Love. Love. Love. The Father's love. Holy Spirit's love. Our love.

Why did you do this for me?

So you could experience all of Me. So we could be together now, Me speaking and you listening. I also did it for your healing; for you to know that by My own death and resurrection NOTHING, ABSOLUTELY NOTHING is too dead, too rotten, too broken in your life for Me to resurrect. My body was dead for three days! That's bad! If the Holy Spirit could do that to My physical body believe He is willing to do it for your body, for your life. Believe! Nothing is too dead! Believe! Do you believe?

Yes, Lord Jesus

Just as I, by the power of the Holy Spirit, rolled the stone away, you roll the stones away. Those are the obstacles blocking your path. The stone says, "you can't get outta here", and you move those stones by the power of My Spirit and by the help of My angels. Go!

161

- **Enjoy Being with Me... (Anonymous)**

We are walking and the Father is holding my hand as we walked, I was walking on a log. There were lots of twigs and bark all around from the storm which was over. I was wearing a dress with black patent leather shoes trying not to get dirty but there was lots of mud around from the storm.

Jesus's eyes were watching. I looked up at Him. He was very tall and I was very sure-footed as He held My hand. I didn't want to walk in the mud so He picked me up and walked toward the water. He didn't care that my shoes were dirty, and I could get dirt on his long white linen robe. I like that He was holding me, and I didn't want to get down. We were walking on the dock and we walk halfway and sat on the bench.

We were watching the boats go by. It was afternoon. "Why are we just sitting? Let's go," I said. He said, *"you need to learn to be still. You don't have to always be doing something. Listen to the birds. Look at that one. He's watching you. It was on a post and I could hear it screeching."*

"What are you trying to tell me, Lord?" He said: *"You are so busy wasting time that you're not taking time for what's important. It's not that hard to hear My voice. You have to stop and listen. Enjoy being with Me. I'll give you a song."*

I heard a melody and was trying to think of the words. ♪♫
I'm coming back to the heart of worship and it's all about you Lord, it's all about you. I'm sorry Lord for the things I've made it but it's all about you Jesus[23].

"Yes, if you want to be close to Me you're going to have to just stop and be with Me and I'll let you experience Me. I slowed you down when you were doing too much and that's why

---

23   Song lyrics referencing *The Heart of Worship"* by Michael W. Smith.

your knee went out. But now watching TV is just a mindless distraction. You're so engaged with stories with happy endings that make you feel good. I want to make you not just feel good but satisfy you like never before."

Yes, you do satisfy, and I want more of you and I want to go deeper. I heard Him say; "Read Matthew 22." I wasn't sure it was Jesus, but I turned there. I was amazed! The story is about Jesus telling about the king who prepared a wedding feast for his son and many were invited but those invited didn't come. Jesus says *"Yes you see the choice meats have been cooked and everything is ready but the guests that were invited ignored the invitation and went about their business. Isn't that what you're doing? I want to be involved in your life and have personal time with you. So, you have to come so I can Speak to your heart. Yes, it is all about Me. But it's Me who will satisfy your soul. Come and experience a deeper walk with Me.*

I'm so speechless that you put Matthew 22 in my heart to read. I confess Lord that I was doubting you. So, I think that is what has been holding me back as I journaled this way. Lord I believe, help my unbelief. Psalm 34 comes to mind and again Lord I'm wondering if it's you and it says I will praise the Lord at all times. I will constantly speak his praises. I will boast only in the Lord.

Jesus says, *"Say that again?"*

I will boast only in the Lord.

Yes, that's what I want you to do, boast in Me. Taste and see that I am good. Oh, the joys of those who trust in Me. Have you tasted My goodness? There is so much more. See the vast lake in front of you? More water than you can see. I Am the living waters. I want to give you more and more fresh experiences with Me. Will you come so I can show you. Put Me first. Run into my arms. I will never let you go My child.

I love you. I will lead you because I Am your Shepherd. Now go praise and boast in Me.

- **Hang gliding with Jesus, the Friend... (Monica Hoffmann)**

I was standing as my child self on the top of the hill, woods to the left of me in a small lake down to the right. Jesus came behind me with a hang glider. I was so excited to see the hang glider, but mostly to see that Jesus showed up! I wept to see Him. And while the thought of riding a hang glider appealed to me, I could not put myself together at the thought that Jesus was with Me.

So, He put down the hang glider, crouched down, and held Me until I stopped crying. Then I climbed onto His back, my arms wrapped around His neck and we were taking off on the hang glider. We flew down to the lake below, swooping over the water.

The glider disappeared and we Danced across the top of the waves top speed, arms flapping water splashing like Gene Kelly in *Singing in the Rain.*

- **Fullness of Joy ... (Mike Bastien)**

May 18.2020, Lord, I want to be filled full of faith in the Holy Ghost. What do you want to say to me during this time of seclusion?

I wait to be wanted. It is the hungry and thirsty that will be filled. It is not for the halfhearted. It is for those that see the need for more. More of Me, more of My Spirit. It is the strong delight of My heart to give all that is Mine and to watch My children enjoy the fullness of My joy and all that is stored up in My kingdom warehouse. They are just waiting to be wanted and received and taken.

Do you know son, that there is NOT one desire for Me that is not from Me? You cannot want Me without Me depositing that hunger and thirst for more.

In My Presence, there is fullness of joy. It is nowhere else. You cannot find it in the world. You cannot find it in your wife. You cannot find it in the ministry that I have called you too. It is in MY presence. Pursue Me. Look to Me. See Me. Be caught up in Me and what I am saying and seeing for you.

The call is upward and onward. The call is to forget those things that are behind and to press forward to the highest calling. I so delight in filling you and My people with Me and the fullness of My Spirit. There is no greater joy for you or Me. I have paid a great price so that all that is Mine, now becomes yours. It grieves Me deeply when I see My people living with so little, and not experiencing the treasures of My Kingdom.

- **Chasing the Word... (Cindy Feibig)**

I see our meadow and our tree. God is taking me by the hand and leading me over to it. We are sitting down on the blanket under it. Jesus, it looks like you have a plastic bucket, the kind they use to collect money in church. What is it?

I love you, Cindy. This is My special prize for you. I have enough for all your needs and some of your wishes, too. All you have to do is ask Me. I AM always here, so all you have to do is ask Me. Let's play in the meadow.

I see us running around in circles, and You are chasing me. You caught me we are both laughing. I see You throw a frisbee, and I run after it and pick it up. And bring it back to You. What is this?

165

This is how My Word works. I toss it into your life, you run after it. When you pick it up and bring it back to Me, I bless you with it.

I don't understand.

Let Me show you. I present to you My Word about healing. I toss it out into your life. Are you going to chase after?

Lord, it doesn't look like anything special to me. Why not?

You aren't seeing it the way I see it. It's very special. It cost Me My life to give it to you. Now, let's try again. I picked up My Word that you need, about healing, and I throw it into your life. Are you going to get it?

Yes, Lord. Please put in my heart the value of your Word.

I will. Now, are you going to chase after it?

Yes, Lord. I see myself front into the field and pick it up. Look at it turns into a giant bunch of flowers! I pick up the armload of flowers and carry them back to You.

There, that's better. Now can you smell the flowers?

Oh, they smell so pretty, and the pedals are so soft. I bury my face in the flowers.

Now, whenever you feel bad, or you feel sick, remember to smell the flowers. I gave you these flowers to help you feel better. I want you to be well for Me so I can take you with Me where I want you to go. I want you to always be with Me. I will always stay with you. I will never leave or forsake you.

I climbed upon Jesus's lap. I don't have a question. I just want to be with You. I laid my head against his shoulder He hugged me, and I felt safe.

Cindy, I love you. Yes, you are safe here with Me. You don't ever have to leave. Did you know that? You don't ever have to leave My Everlasting Arms.

- **Bridal Chamber Key – (Jacqueline Puliafico)**

    I (saw) an old wooden door, and I had an old fashion key in my hand, and there was my hand and Jesus' hand over mine, and we placed the key in the keyhole and turned the key together.

    The door opened, and the light was extremely bright, I couldn't see anything beyond the light, but I heard *"Abide in Me" I looked up John 15:4 "Remain in Me, and I [will remain] in you. Just as no branch can bear fruit by itself without remaining in the vine, neither can you [bear fruit, producing evidence of your faith] unless you remain in Me."*

Keep the Encounters Going

Go back and encounter God again. Keep allowing God to expand your special place by looking more closely so He can show you what He has added there. Continue to build memories with Him as the:

- Heavenly Father
- Savior
- Immanuel
- Bridegroom
- Friend

Allow Him to direct which Name(s) you most need to build more memories with. Remember what it felt like to connect with Him as each of these Names. Go back and meet Him again as those Names so you begin to have more memories of experiences with Him as those Names. The more memories you have with Him the easier it is to call on those Names when you need Him.

I encourage you to thoroughly review all the Appendix Extras for more on how to Dialogue journal and teach others how to as well.

God bless you and your incredible journey with the Names of God!

Appendix A
Dialogue Journaling Tips

Know which voice you are hearing

- **God's Voice– spontaneous positive** thoughts, pictures, and feelings consistent with any Name of God, Character of God, or Nature of God. (Any of the Fruit of the Spirit, "Omni" truths, and compound Names of God). God can speak through images, stories, emotions and music and sparks of creative insight... God speaks the language of the heart.

- **Satan's voice– spontaneous negative** thoughts, pictures, and feelings consistent with his character and nature. (Lying, deceiving, tears down, lead you away from faith in God). Listening to this voice will lead to faith in reverse and will amplify worry.

- **Your own thoughts – analytical, practical, logical**. Your thoughts speak in the language of the head. They may even look like a list of practical concerns, but remember, the LORD offers solutions.

Don't expect it to look or sound a certain way. God's ways are different from your ways. Your specific expectations can be a significant barrier to hearing from God. He does not need to sound like a booming voice.

Give God credit for when He speaks to you or shows you something spontaneously. That brilliant idea that came to you in the meeting, for example, was God. Make sure you thank Him for it. Likewise, **don't take credit for negative thoughts** or pictures that are self-deprecating or send you backwards in your faith. Those thoughts are from the enemy and the sooner you recognize them and rebuke the enemy out loud, the faster they will cease. Rebuking out loud is important because the enemy is not Omniscient. He doesn't know your thoughts. So, speak with the authority of God when you recognize these negative messages.

Have **spiritual counselors** to help you make sure you are hearing from God. The characteristics of a good spiritual counselor are:

- They should **know the Word, have a close relationship with God, be able to discern His Voice themselves. They should also be humble enough to have spiritual advisors themselves.**

- **Submit your journaling** to a counselor when **you are learning** how to discern God's voice.

- **Submit your journaling** to a counselor to **people with more experience** in an area where you have specific issues for which the LORD is addressing.

- **Submit your journaling** to a counselor when you get a message **that does not seem consistent with God's**

170

Character. Remember, God's Voice will be full of faith, hope, and love. He will gently and lovingly convict of sin but will not condemn or tear you down.

• **Submit your journaling** to a counselor if it is related to a **major life transition, or you feel that what you received doesn't feel or sound like God.**

Don't try – Striving to hear from God is you trying in your own effort. This does not work, and you will likely get a journal that analyzes your circumstances logically. This is not from God. You need to relax **and let God take the wheel**. It's much easier than you might expect.

Imagine yourself as a small child. This connects you with your inner child and **awakens childlike faith**.

It doesn't have to be perfect. Don't put off talking to God because you want everything to be perfect and you want to have a lot of time to do it. **It doesn't require a lot of time** to speak to Jesus. A few minutes of quality time with Jesus is much better than not spending time with Him at all.

Avoid evaluating what you are receiving from the LORD as you are getting it. **Evaluation in the moment is doubt.** When you begin to doubt the validity of the experience, you hang up on Jesus. Allow yourself to receive the flow of the Holy Spirit freely, knowing you can evaluate it later.

Evaluate what you have received after your time with Jesus is complete. The message should be consistent with Scripture and the Names and Character of God. God is all about faith, hope and love. Even if the Lord is giving you constructive discipline, your message from the LORD should build you up, help you feel loved and give you hope. If it doesn't, then it's worth passing by a spiritual counselor.

How to avoid distractions

Internal distractions like having a lot of things on your mind can be dealt with by pulling out paper and **writing a list of the things that you need to do** so you won't forget them. That way you can literally set them aside and focus on the LORD.

External distractions – Find a place where you know that no one will bother you. If necessary, use noise canceling earphones or relaxation music with no crescendos. And, no one bothers you in the bathtub. ;-)

Ways to quiet yourself down

Deep breathing- Breathe in the Power of the Holy Spirit, exhale anxiety and other negative thoughts. It's relaxing and helps you focus on Jesus.

Find a **comfortable place and position**- Don't get so comfortable that you fall asleep. Although, God certainly can and does speak to us in dreams! Comfortable means that you are not distracted by pain but are not so relaxed that you fall asleep.

If **music** is helpful, that's great. Just make sure that it is **instrumental and has a steady rhythm**. You don't want the music to lead the experience. That's Jesus' job. The songs in this book are more for worship and meditation which posture your heart for connecting with God. For quiet meditation, however, go with relaxing instrumental songs. I find that "Classic Music for Studying" and "Instrumental Christian" are great Pandora[24] stations for journaling.

Singing or praying in tongues is a wonderful way to get your eyes on Jesus. When you have surrendered your mouth, you can know that the Holy Spirit is fully engaged, and your heart is made ready for Jesus. It is a guaranteed way to make sure that Jesus is taking the wheel. However, if this is not a gift that God has released in you yet, do *not* stress about it or feel that God is not speaking to you. Ask God to open the door for the gift of tongues to be released in you. He will answer that prayer.

Capturing the flow of the Holy Spirit

Always begin by **fixing your eyes on Jesus**. It's OK if you don't see Jesus' face or whole body at first. That is common. But don't let that make you think it's not real or isn't working. Sometimes people can just feel His loving Presence and that's enough. The point is that **He needs to be your focus.**

Speak with and experience only the One True God. Don't pray to your deceased relatives, or any other entities. You are speaking to the Father through Jesus, by the power of the Holy Spirit. You can call directly to any Names of the Godhead (Jesus, Heavenly Father, Holy Spirit, or any of God's Names), just don't pray to or worship anyone else.

I encourage you to set the stage of your conversation with Jesus by meeting with Him in **your special place**, for example. But once He is in the scene, **take your hands off the wheel and let Him take over**. The purpose of the special place is to give you an anchoring place to

---

24 www.Pandora.com

collect memories of Jesus that make it easier to trust that you can see Him again there whenever you need to. You don't need to always see Him there, however. And, God can change your special place over time.

Some people can and like to **write down the conversation** as it is happening. I do this. It's just capturing what the LORD is saying as He is saying it. This is especially important if you are using the ears of your heart to hear Him speak. **Others need to see the scene without pulling out the paper and writing.** When I ask God for a visual experience, I do this. If this is you, then make sure to ask the LORD to help you remember everything that is important so you can write it down afterwards. I want to keep looking and the LORD is faithful to help me remember every detail that I experienced. When the vision is complete, I journal what I saw.

Writing your journal conversations and experiences is important, even if you don't like writing. Your journal provides a **written record** of what the LORD has said and shown you. It is also a log **of your answered prayers**. I always re-read my journals when they are full and it's amazing to remember the experiences I had with Jesus that I may have forgotten.

Remember that this is **a conversation with God**, keep looking, keep talking, and **ask follow-up questions** like you would if you were talking to a friend. Write down the flow of that conversation.

A **song** rolling around in your head can be a message from God. I like to look up the lyrics of a song that is stuck in my head. There is nearly always a message in the lyrics that is exactly what I needed that day.

What to do when you are stuck

Watch how you talk about being stuck. Don't activate faith in reverse by saying out loud that "I can't do this." You can do it; you just need to believe that you can do it because the LORD promises that everyone can do it. **Speak in agreement with what God says.**

Confess and repent any unbelief and ask God to increase your faith so that you can relax and be able to hear and see Him.

Ask the LORD if there is any unconfessed sin that may be blocking your ability to hear. **Confess and repent of that sin** and try it again.

If you are still stuck, fast and **pray for the LORD to show you** the specific block. You may have a feeling, or a person's name pop in your mind, or a conflict that needs to be addressed. Listen and do what He says to get the flow back.

Things to avoid

God is not a genie or a magic 8 ball. For this reason, **avoid asking predictive questions** about your future. The LORD will reveal promises and glimpses of your future when and if He desires. Trust Him one day at a time. Ask Him about today. Matthew 6:11 says; "Give us this day."

Along the same lines, **avoid telling Jesus how you want things to go,** or what you think should happen. This is a learning curve for sure, but things will go much better for you when you learn to let God take control. Keep your attitude humble and faithful.

Great Questions to Ask Jesus

It is helpful to focus your prayer by **calling on the Name of God** that is related to your issue: Some examples are:

- Jehovah Jireh, how can I cooperate with your prvision.

- Good Shepherd, what do you want me to do today?

- Comforter, you know every heart and every motivation, show me their heart. Or, Show me my heart.

- Great I AM, You are the Source of all wisdom, please give me wisdom in this circumstance.

- Mighty Counselor, You know that very best course of action for this circumstance; what do you want me to say or do in this situation today?

- LORD, you are the Author of my story, what is the step I can take today to move forward toward the promise you have given me?

- Great Physician what do I need to do to receive your healing? What is the condition that I need to meet to receive healing?

- Word of God, help me understand these Scripture verses. No one can explain them better than He can.

- Ask Jesus about Biblical concepts like, Abiding in Him, Forgiveness, Surrender, Old Testament concepts and their New Testament parallels, The Trinity, Creation, etc. Anything you want to understand more about your faith, the Bible, and your relationship with Him is OK to ask. He is not too busy to answer these questions. In fact, He delights in answering them.

Pour your heart out to God. You can be brutally honest with God. He knows everything anyway. There's no point in trying to be phony with God. Your best friend wouldn't put up with that, so why should Jesus? After you vent, make sure you pause and listen. This is what made King David the man after God's own heart.

Remember to **let Jesus do most of the talking**. If your journals are filled with your venting and no responses from Jesus, you are missing a huge blessing. This is "dialogue journaling", not "monologue journaling." Dialogue journaling is your prayers with God's response in conversations and experiences. What He has to say is the more important part of the conversation. Also, when the Lord pours His heart out to you, thank Him. **Reply to Him that you understand what He is saying and purpose in your spirit to obey Him.**

Adventures to have with Jesus

- **Enter a Bible scene**- If you have read about an experience that someone had in the Bible, you can ask Jesus to give you this experience. A few nice ones that I have had the pleasure of experiencing were talking with Jesus at the well, walking on water, listening to Jesus give the Sermon on the Mount, and watching David write a psalm. The Bible is full of wonderful stories and Jesus loves to take us on adventures.

- **A shared Bible story experience**- The above idea can also be experienced as a group. My Bible study group experienced the Day of Pentecost by meditating together on Acts 1:1-21. The LORD showed each of us something different and we shared what we saw as we were prompted by Him to do so. Our experiences rounded out a beautiful picture together!

- **Jesus will often take you on adventures** without you asking for them. If He wants you to understand something, He will take you to a place and allow you to experience an activity that will send the exact message that He has for you. **Be willing to follow Him on that adventure.**

- A great healing opportunity is to **ask Jesus to take you to a difficult time in your past** and asking Him to show you either where He was at the time, or give you His perspective on it. Just seeing Him there can be all it takes to lead you to forgiveness.

- **Ask the LORD to give you a picture, story, metaphor, or parable** that will help you understand a Biblical concept or a complicated situation you are facing. This is exactly how Jesus taught people while He was on earth. So, we know that He loves to do that and will do that for you as you work through the encounter exercises in this book. He speaks in your personal language and brings in elements from your own life to help you understand things.

How to call on the Names and Promises of God

The easiest way to find anything in the Bible is to simply put the search term in any computer browser. If you want scripture about healing, simply putting 'verses about healing' for example. I guarantee many people have already written blogs or created lists on this topic for you! If you want to find a Bible story, simply type a search word about is such as 'verses walking on water' and the verses about Peter's experience will pop up.

For a more in-depth Biblical study, BibleGateway.com has advanced search capacity. In addition to just putting in a keyword, verse or topic in the main search bar, there is a "keyword search" just below that bar that allows you to search 3 ways: **match all words, match any word, match exact phrase.** I will indicate below which of those matching keywords that I used to come up with the recommended lists accordingly. Play around with this capability. The more specific you are in your keyword search, the more results that match what you are actually looking for will come up.

You may also play around with parallel scriptures or do these search terms with different Bible versions. The app and website have wonderful flexibility.

Finding the Name of God in Scripture:

Perhaps the best overall search for the Names of God is to **search "God is"** (exact phrase). This will give you 1376 verses in the NIV and is a wonderful way to learn in much more detail about the "Is-ness" of God.

- Example: 1 John 4:16 "And so we know and rely on the love God has for us. **God is love.** Whoever lives in love lives in God, and God in them."

  Along those lines, the search **"I am"** will return 967 verses in the NIV (exact word order search).

- Example: Genesis 17:1 "When Abram was ninety-nine years old, the LORD appeared to him and said, "**I am God Almighty**; walk before me faithfully and be blameless.""

Look for the intention of the Scripture. The verse doesn't need to include the Name of God in it to address the topics or areas of concern under the Name's jurisdiction. **Ask, "What is the key action of this Scripture?"**

- Example: Jeremiah 30:17 "For I will restore you to health And I will heal you of your wounds,' declares the LORD..." The key action of this verse is to restore health and heal wound. The Great Physician is the Name of God for this verse.

To look for the Name of God, I **look at the key action or character** represented in the verse. Is the verse trying to give me comfort? Then the Name of God may be the Comforter. Is the verse giving me wisdom or advice? Then it's probably the Mighty Counselor that is speaking. Is God fighting for me in this verse? Then it may be addressing the Shield, the Banner, or the Mighty Warrior. Is the verse suggesting leading us in a certain direction or giving us guidance in our lives? Perhaps it is referencing the Good Shepherd or the Author. If it's about physical, emotional, mental or physical needs, then it could be addressing the Great Physician and Healer.

Finding the Promises of God:

To look for a promise in the Bible **look for absolute words** such as 'will', 'always', 'forever' or 'never', as opposed to 'sometimes', 'might' kinds of statements. There are a lot of absolute words in the Bible if you look for them.

- Example: Deuteronomy 31:6 Be strong and courageous. Do not be afraid or terrified because of them, for the LORD your God goes with you; he **will never leave you nor forsake you**." The promise here is that the LORD will never leave or forsake you!

Searching (all words search) **'promises, God'**. 80 verses will pop up for you in the NIV. Or (all words search) **'covenant, God'** and 81 verses will pop up for that one.

- Example: Psalm 85:8 "I will listen to what **God** the LORD says; He **promises** peace to His people, His faithful servants— but let them not turn to folly."

Finding the Conditions of the Promise:

When looking for conditions of a promise, search for words like **"if,"** **"when," "then"** kinds of words.

- Example: 2 Chronicles 7:14 "**if** my people, who are called by my Name, will humble themselves and pray and seek my face and turn from their wicked ways, **then** I will hear from heaven, and I will forgive their sin and will heal their land." Humility, seeking God's face and turning from wicked ways are the conditions required for the promise of healing their land.

"Therefore" is a word that tells me that I need to look for the **context of a promise** or a command. Whenever you see the word, "therefore," ask God, what is that "there for"? Look a verse or two before to find the context when the word "therefore" is present.

- Example: Matthew 19:67 "So they are no longer two, but one flesh. What **therefore** God has joined together, let no man separate." The unity of the two becoming one flesh is the context for the command for no man to separate them.

Noticing when the conditions are commands.

A **command is directive language**. You can tell a directive when it begins the sentence and directives are usually commanding verbs. It is intentional and strong.

- Example: Matthew 7:7 "**Ask**, and it **will** be given to you; **seek**, and you **will** find; **knock**, and it **will** be opened to you...." Ask, seek, and knock are the directives. The three uses of "will" show you to the promises.

Notice that the directives are also the conditions of the promise. You need to cooperate with the Holy Spirit in this verse to receive these promises.

How to pray with authority/without idols in your heart

- Before you pray, do some **Bible research** based on your issue and need. Using the tips above, find the Name, characteristic or topic to research and find His promises categorically.

- **Call on the Name of God** relevant to your circumstance or issue.

- **Praise Him** for what that Name means for this situation.

- **Remind Him Who He is** and what He has promised.

- **Confess and repent** of any anxiety or unbelief that He can take care of in this situation.

- **Speak out loud that you agree with God**'s best plan and His sovereignty in this situation.

- **Ask Him to show you what the conditions** are for the healing or issue to be resolved.

- Obey His instructions.

- **Thank Him** for what you will learn and for how He will resolve this situation.

- **Praise Him** and end with "In Jesus' Name, Amen." This is important because you are claiming the authority of Jesus when you pray.

Practice this by taking any of the Names of God in this list and using the Scripture and promised identified, or what you have learned from researching the other search recommendations, write out a prayer that addresses your issue.

Example situation: You have just lost your job unexpectedly and have anxiety about the bills. You want peace in your heart. An example prayer is below the Name listing:

Prince of Peace

Found in: Philippians 4:6-7 ⁶"Do not be anxious about anything, but in every situation, by prayer and petition, with thanksgiving, present your requests to God. ⁷And the peace of God, which transcends all understanding, will guard your hearts and your minds in Christ Jesus."

Promises made by this Name: Peace is part of the Fruit of the Spirit. We can't have it without God. The LORD wouldn't command us not to be anxious if it was impossible. He gives us the instructions in these verses. Surrender all to Him and He will give you peace!

Other Verses or Search Terms

- Isaiah 9:6

- Ephesians 2:11-18

- John 14:27

- John 16:33

- Galatians 5:22

- Peace, God- 42 verses

- Peace, Spirit- 9 verses

- Peace, Jesus- 27 verses

Your Turn Practice Exercises:

Example Prayer: LORD, you are my Prince of Peace. You know that I have lost my job, and You have commanded me not to be anxious. You promise me that You will give me peace in all situations. I thank You for this turn of events because I trust that you are guarding my heart against fear and will bless me with Your Peace in this circumstance. I surrender this situation to You and trust You to guide me in Your Peace. What do You want me to know or to do today to receive Your Peace in this situation? Let the peace that transcends all understanding wash over me. I thank You and praise You, In Jesus Name, Amen.

1. Practice praying this same situation over using another Name from the list. Perhaps the Author, Shepherd or Provider would be a good start.

2. Now choose an issue that is relevant to you, choose a Name from the chart and practice this prayer on your own issue.

3. How do you feel now that you prayed this way?

Bible Resources Online

- YouVersion is a resource that will help you stay in the Word. It's a Bible app you can download from any app store for your mobile devices and by www.youversion.com on your computer. You can **read, listen to and watch videos of the Bible in more versions than you even knew existed**. Bible reading plans help me **read the Bible every day**. Other app capabilities include parallel versions, notes, create verse images and post Bible verses on social media.

- BibleGateway is an app and great website resource for Scripture searches. It has **advanced search capabilities** that allow you to filter your search by offering a variety of specific filters such as languages, topic, match categories (such as exact phrase, all words, or any word) and side by side parallel versions. Download it in your app store or visit www.Biblegateway.com.

- Biblehub is for the serious Bible researcher. Just about every Bible study resource can be found in this app and website. Once you type a verse on the home search screen you find on that same results page, the Scripture in context (one verse before and one after), **parallel versions, cross references, and commentaries**. There are simply too many features of this app to mention, but this one is great when you really want to dive into the Word and **research from many different angles**. Check out www.Biblehub.com.

- The Web Bible Encyclopedia by ChristianAnswers.net has a dictionary of **939 Names and Titles of God** with links to Scriptures that reference them. They are also distinguished by Hebrew, Greek, Aramaic and Latin. You can use the Bible research tools below to dive into any of them on this site. http://www.christiananswers.net/dictionary/namesofgod.html

Appendix B

Salvation Prayer

❧

Acts 10:36 reminds us that Jesus is LORD of all. That means that He is LORD of everyone, not only those who accept His gift of salvation and become children of God. It's another absolute truth of God. Some will realize that for the first time on Judgement Day when we will all experience Romans 14:11 "As surely as I live, says the LORD, every knee will bend to Me, and every tongue will confess and give praise to God." So then, each of us will give an account of ourselves to God.

Still, for those that choose to accept the gift of salvation, we have the right to become children of God.

> John 1:12 (NIV) Yet to all who did receive him, to those who believed in his Name, he gave the right to become children of God.

We have the power to share in God's divine nature and character and truly live the lives that He has planned for us from the beginning of time.

Jeremiah 29:11-14 (NIV) [11]For I know the plans I have for you," declares the LORD, "plans to prosper you and not to harm you, plans to give you hope and a future. [12]Then you will call on me and come and pray to me, and I will listen to you. [13]You will seek me and find me when you seek me with all your heart. 14I will be found by you," declares the LORD, "and will bring you back from captivity."

If you haven't accepted Christ's gift of salvation and you are ready to do that, it's really simple. Just have a conversation with Jesus, and He will hear your heart cry. Admit that you need Jesus. Ask God for forgiveness. Believe that Jesus came to save you. Accept the free gift. Confess with your mouth that you receive the gift. Thank Him for saving you. There are no magic words to make that happen. He will accept your heartfelt prayer and send the Holy Spirit to dwell in your heart. It's that simple.

It could go something like this: Jesus, I'm tired of living my life without you. Forgive me for all my sins and for trying to do this life on my own without You. I need You to come and help me. I believe that You are who you say You are, Jesus. Thank you for offering me the way to eternal life. Come into my life now and show me how to be my best self, LORD. Thank you for sending me the Holy Spirit to show me the Way.

Once you have sincerely prayed a prayer like this, you are saved. Congratulations and welcome to the family!

Appendix C
How to Teach People to Journal

*I*f learning how to journal has changed your relationship with God and your life, and you want others to know how simple it is, please follow these simple steps so you can teach people how to connect with God like you can. This process can take only 30 minutes; with 15 minutes to explain it, and 15 minutes to experience God and discuss it.

1. **Induce Hunger-*Why should people want to know how to hear God's voice personally?***

   b. MOST IMPORTANTLY- Share your own story of how using this tool has changed your relationship with the Lord and changed your life. If you have a journal example you would like to share, that is usually what makes people want to try it!

   c. Ask them; Would you like to have the God who created heaven and earth speak to you by name about issues in your life; show you how to solve your problems, explain the Bible to you, give you direction, and personally heal you?

d. Explain that the Names of God are personal, such as the Bridegroom, Mighty Counselor, Friend, Defender, Provider, Healer. Would you marry, seek counseling, trust with your secrets, and lean on when you were in crisis, someone you can't see, hear or feel? God has these Names because He showed up as these Names to people in the Bible and they personally encountered Him in these ways. So can you.

2. **Normalize it- *Hearing from God is normal and easy.***

a. God created everyone to see and hear Him with the eyes and ears of their heart. If you were unable to do so, you would never have accepted Him as your Savior in the first place. God is not willing for ANY to perish, so He wired us to be able to communicate with Him.

b. The entire Bible was written using the same four keys I will teach you in a few minutes.

c. Two-thirds of the Bible came to people who heard from God and they wrote it down and one-third of the Bible came when people received messages from the Lord by dreams and visions and they wrote it down. In all cases, they were using the ears and eyes of their hearts to connect with God.

d. God is the same yesterday, today and forever (Hebrews 13:8). So, if this is how He spoke to Bible writers, He can do it now too. Even more so now that we have the Holy Spirit whose job is to endue us with the power to connect with God's nature and release His love to others. This direct access to Father God is what Jesus accomplished for us on the cross.

3. **Address New Age Concern upfront-** *It is different than what the New Agers do...*

   a. When you ask for Jesus, you get Jesus. Matthew 7:9-11 New American Standard Bible (NASB)[9] Or what man is there among you [a]who, when his son asks for a loaf, [b]will give him a stone? [10] Or [c] if he asks for a fish, he will not give him a snake, will he? [11] If you then, being evil, know how to give good gifts to your children, how much more will your Father who is in heaven give what is good to those who ask Him.

   b. New Agers seek generalized spiritual realm and they get negative spirits.

   c. We **can** know which voice-

      i. God sounds like His Names and character (fruit of the Spirit, build you up, encourage and edify, disciplines lovingly but does not condemn).

      ii. The enemy sounds like his names and character (lies, deceit, tears down, robs, steals, destroys, condemns). Condemnation speaks in generalities and results in guilt, shame, and negative identity whereas conviction is specific loving feedback and leads to repentance, healing, and restoration.

      iii. Your voice is logical and analytical and is limited to a natural world understanding.

4. **Share the Four Keys to Hearing God's Voice-** *There are four simple steps to hearing God's voice.*

a. **Quiet yourself down**- Externally and internally

b. **Fix your Eyes on Jesus**... ask and expect to see, hear, feel from Him

c. **Tune to spontaneity**- allow the pictures, thoughts, feelings to bubble up... don't try too hard

d. Write down what you saw, heard and felt,

These steps can be seen in action in Habakkuk 2:1-2

Verse segment	How it relates to the 4 Keys
[1]I will stand on my guard post And station myself on the rampart;	He found a quiet place so he could look up to God. He was posturing his heart to speak to God Himself.
And I will keep watch to see what He will speak to me,	He was looking and listening with an expectation to hear from God personally... using the eyes and ears of his heart.
And how I may reply when I am reproved.	Habakkuk knew it would be a conversation with God. He knew that he could be able to hear what God had to say AND that he could reply.
[2]Then the LORD answered me and said,	God did reply personally.
"Record the vision and inscribe *it* on tablets, That the one who reads it may run.	God commanded Habakkuk to write down what He was going to say... writing it down is not just for you to be able to remember, but it can also be a blessing for others.

5. **Preparing for your first Jesus Encounter-**

a. Manage expectations--- God's voice sounds like your own thoughts and pictures on the screen of your mind but spontaneously and with His character... it's a bit more loving than you are usually.

b. Practice seeing with the eyes of your heart. Close your eyes and picture your kitchen or bedroom of your house. Look around the room using the eyes of your heart. The clarity of the picture in your mind is the clarity of the image you will likely see when you go to see Jesus. So, it is not as clear as what you can see with your natural eyes, but you can still get an impression of what you are sensing.

c. Practice hearing with the ears of your heart by closing your eyes and singing the Happy Birthday song in your mind.

d. Some see easier and others hear easier, others get feelings. All of these are good beginnings. So, be happy with what you experience. All of us have these senses so, even if you are not experiencing all of them at first, you can ask God to give you an increased sensitivity and practice. You will get better at it. So, don't despise small beginnings.

e. Encourage them to imagine themselves as a child between the ages of 4 to 8 as this will help connect them to God with a more open heart because it activates their childlike faith.

6. **The Special Place-** *Have a special place in your spirit where you can go to and see Jesus there anytime.*

a. This short, guided imagery will take you to a place of God's choosing for you to meet with Him. http://bit.ly/2g8v8iu

b. How this guided imagery works, so you can facilitate something like it if you prefer.

    i. Imagine a beautiful place. For some it will be a place that they have been where there are loving memories. For others, it is a beautiful place in general or even a supernatural place. The Lord knows exactly what place to pop into people's minds. Do not direct what this looks like. Relax and let the image pop into your mind. God speaks in your language, so even if it seems strange at first, go with it.

    ii. Wake up and activate the Right-brain by asking them to see, hear, smell, feel this place, left, front, right, up, and down. Speak it slowly enough for them to take in some details. This part is to make sure they are waking up their spiritual senses even before we introduce Jesus to the scene. Again, do not tell them what to see here, just tell them to look, listen.

    iii. Then ask them to turn around and see Jesus walking toward them. He has a smile on His face. When He approaches, He hugs them. This is specifically, so they see Jesus as His loving character.

    iv. The first question that we recommend that they ask Jesus is "How do You feel about Me"? Then, completely take your hand off the wheel and let Jesus take it from there.

c. Give them time. Eight to ten minutes is usually a good amount of time. Then ask them to share their experience. If you are giving them the link above and they are not doing it now, schedule a time to review their first journal. This increases the likelihood that they do it.

d. Encourage them in their experience. This was a REAL Jesus encounter, not a figment of their imagination. Tell them that they can go back to the special place ANYTIME and Jesus will be there for them again.

Appendix D
Shepherd's Two-Ways

❦

Experiencing these two opportunities to see what the shepherds saw on the night of Jesus' birth has forever changed my heart posture for Christmas. Every time I hear a Christmas song about the shepherds and baby Jesus, I remember these encounters. I hope you take the same journey as you read these two stories. One from mine and the other from one of the shepherd's perspective.

My Visionary Encounter of the Night of Jesus' Birth

It was a few days before Christmas, and I was praying in the Spirit. I wanted a deeper sense of the true meaning of Christmas, so I asked the Lord to show me what the shepherds saw on the night that Jesus was born.

Suddenly, my guardian angel Maureen and I were standing next to five Shepherd boys who were sleeping around a fire. I felt like Scrooge in *A Christmas Carol*; there but not really there, watching the story unfold. Lit only by the stars and the moon, I could see their young dirty faces, wrapped tightly in sheepskin wooly mantles, fighting to stay warm in the cool of the night. "They're kids!" I whispered to Maureen as if I could wake them by speaking. "They look like they are only 11-16 years old." She nodded and smiled.

There were hundreds of sheep, some bleating, some quietly sleeping, all packed together in a large group. Another shepherd was leaning against a tree, keeping watch. When suddenly, a bright angel appeared in the sky and started moving toward him. The watchman ran quickly over to the others who were waking from the bright light of the angel. Some were trembling, another was crying as this angel spoke to them in their own language. I didn't understand what was being said, but I had a good idea, having read the story in Scripture many times about the night of Jesus' birth and this encounter with the shepherds.

Suddenly, the sky was full of an immeasurable number of bright angels. The light of them lit up the pasture like daylight. As they sang praises to the Lord, it sounded like ocean waves; rhythmic and beautiful. It was hypnotically moving. I could have listened to this sound forever.

Then abruptly, like a vortex, the singing angels were swept away and only the original angel and a few others remained. The angel gave the boys instructions and guided them along a road while the few angels stayed to mind the sheep. Maureen and I watched as the group walked through the moonlit streets of Bethlehem guided by the angel. "Were you one of those singing angels?" I asked Maureen. "No, each of us have different jobs, and singing is not mine!" she giggled. "But I'm happy to be here to see it with you!" I smiled gratefully.

The vision popped like a soap bubble, and the next thing I knew, Maureen and I were inside the stable. The first thing I noticed was the smell. It was an overpowering combination of animal waste, sweat, and blood. I covered my nose and squinted my eyes to get used to this new vision. It was a much larger building than I had pictured from my many reference images of this scene. Mary, the new young mother, was sitting on a pile of hay, leaning against a support beam, nursing the baby Jesus. "She looks like a middle school kid", I said to Maureen. "Yes, she is fourteen years old." Maureen clarified. Her hair stuck to her forehead and her face was flushed and glistening with sweat. She was wearing layers of filthy garments. Her teenaged face looked weary, yet grateful and she was smiling at her still messy newborn.

Joseph, the young father, was looking at them with a combination of wonder and anxiety. He was a nice-looking young man with dark olive skin, a short beard, kind eyes, and a gracious manner. I couldn't help but wonder if he was overwhelmed to be chosen as the earthly father of the Messiah. Mary caught his glance and his expression quickly shifted to a loving smile. "He must be terrified of this kind of responsibility", I whispered to Maureen. "No doubt", she said. "But the Father chose him and fully equipped him for the job. He will be a great earthly father for the Messiah" Maureen whispered back.

The baby Jesus had a lot of black hair, olive skin, and the squinty puffiness of birth. He was tightly wrapped in gauze-like cloth strips so the only part of his body that was visible was his tiny content face. The place was much larger than I had pictured and there were camels, goats, and several sheep tied to large metal rings on the walls of the stone room. I wanted to get a closer look at the baby. Even though I knew they couldn't see me, and I wasn't actually intruding on anything, it felt strange to be present for such a private moment. They were so young, and the baby was so important. I wondered if they could grasp the magnitude and significance of this child, they were now responsible for raising.

A knock at the door opening startled the couple and Mary quickly laid the baby Jesus on the scratchy hay of the manger. The baby's bed was a large x-shaped wood and stone animal feeding trough that stretched against the entire wall of the room like a channel. The new family was near the front door opening when Joseph inquired what the shepherds were doing there. The leader of the shepherds answered Joseph's questions and seemed very insistent that they were supposed to be there.

Joseph glanced over at Mary with considerate eyes, explaining to her that angels had told these young men to come and see the newborn King. Joseph gave Mary a look that seemed to be asking her permission to let them come inside. They both looked at each other and shrugged and Joseph stepped aside to allow them in.

Mary blushed and looked away, nervously and embarrassed at the encounter, but allowed the men in the room. With a full belly, the Son of God slept unbothered by the visitors or the discomfort of His scratchy bed and smelly surroundings. The shepherd boys stood at a distance, bowing, and kneeling reverently to the new family. The leader of the group walked up to the manger and asked Joseph's permission to approach the baby. As he bent down to get a closer look and touch the cheek of the new Messiah, a tear streamed down his cheek as he whispered something in the ear of the baby. He wiped his tear quickly and stepped back with the others. This sight touched me greatly and I found myself wiping a tear away as well.

Mary's face grimaced in pain as she smiled graciously at the eldest shepherd. He took the cue that they had overstayed their welcome and they said a prayer of thanksgiving and left the new family alone. On the walk back to the sheepfold, the young men talked about all that they had seen and heard.

When the visions were over, I thanked the Lord for all that He had shown me. I have a new appreciation for the humility of the birth and surroundings and the magnificence of the angels.

I asked, Lord, whatever happened to these shepherds? He answered...

> *All of the shepherds began to share the story of their experience with the Angels and the baby, but only two of them looked and watched for the Messiah. Many years later, these two faithful men heard of Me. They looked for Me and heard Me teaching. They both accepted Me as their Savior. They were faithful to share the stories of their experiences with their families and friends. As a result, they were influential in helping many others come to know Me as well. They lived fruitful lives and enjoy blessings with Me in heaven today!*

> *Not all of the shepherds believed though. It was all so much for them to take in. Over time, they began to think of the experience as more of a dream than reality. This is like the parable of the soils. Some will have hearts that are ripe and ready to receive the Truth, and others will not. The fruit of the two shepherds is still growing to this day! They sought out the truth, believed, and shared it with others. This is all I ask!*

A Shepherd's Experience of the Night of the Messiah's Birth

On a hillside, just outside of Bethlehem, Ezra was leaning against a tree, daydreaming in the moonlight as the sheep bleated quietly in the chill of the night. He was sixteen, the oldest of the shepherds, and was taking his shift to watch these 343 sheep while his twelve-year-old brother Simon and four others were taking their turns sleeping by the fire. It was an especially bright night, as there was a star that seemed larger and brighter than the others. Ezra was looking at that star curiously when a flash of moving light caught his eye. The light stopped right in front of him. It was a winged glowing angel hovering about 15 feet above the ground.

Terrified, he ran to wake up the others, hoping not the upset the flock in the process. The flying angel followed him to the group who was waking up from the light and the commotion. They were paralyzed with fear when the angel told them not to be afraid. He shared that the Messiah that had been promised in the Holy Scriptures had just been born in Bethlehem. He would provide a way for all who believed in Him to be saved. It was a time of great joy for the entire world.

Ezra asked a few questions, trying to understand what was happening so he could help the younger boys understand as well. When suddenly, there was a blinding light and the sky was full of angels glowing and singing praises to the Lord. Ezra had never heard or seen anything so beautiful in his life. Simon clung to his brother's mantel, trembling, and trying to take it all in. The praises from the angels were like rhythmic waves. Ezra found himself swaying unconsciously to the lovely music of it. All the shepherd boys were captivated and overwhelmed by the scene, falling to their knees in humble praise.

Swiftly, like a tornado, the angels were sucked back up to heaven. Not all were whisked away though. There were a few left who promised to watch over the sheep so that Ezra and the other shepherd boys could go find the Messiah. They were told that they would find him lying in a manger in a stable. The angel showed them the way as they walked through the sleepy town of Bethlehem. It had been chaos in the last few days because people in the line of David had to come to this town for the census. But at this hour, the overcrowded town was asleep and had no awareness of their travels or the significance of this baby's birth.

They arrived at the stable for which the angel had directed them, and Ezra timidly approached the door entryway. He stayed outside of the stable but called in to speak to the young father. "I'm so sorry to intrude at this late hour," Ezra said timidly, "And I hope you don't think we are crazy, but we had this angel come to tell us that the Messiah was born here tonight ... I'm sorry, I don't know why he wanted us to come and see this baby..."Ezra looked away embarrassed and then looked back at Joseph with pleading eyes. "But we genuinely want to see this promised Messiah and"... The new father leaned in and whispered to Ezra..."I know about visitations from angels. I believe you, just let me see if it's Ok with my wife. She just had a baby you know." He looked back at the new mother's curious face and explained that an angel had told these shepherds that the baby was the Messiah and they were instructed to come and see Him. They exchanged a look and a shrug that seemed to say, 'as God wishes', and let the young men in the room.

Ezra and the shepherds walked slowly into the stable, careful to keep their distance. They knelt in reverence and for a long time, just stared at the baby. 'He looks so, ordinary', Ezra thought. 'He is just a regular looking baby.' He didn't know why he thought that the baby would look different, but he knew that He **was** different. Bashfully, he approached the manger and knelt. He looked up at the new parents with a 'may I?' look on his face, asking if he could touch the baby. They nodded that it was fine, and he reached his calloused hand up the sleeping baby's cheek and gave it a gentle brush with this forefinger.

Ezra leaned in as if the baby could understand his words and said, "I'm going to be watching for you as you grow up. I'm going to follow you and tell everyone I know about this night. May God's will come true through you exactly as God promised."

Ezra looked up and saw the baby's mother smiling at him. He could see the pain on her face from the recent delivery. It was time to let them have their privacy. Ezra rose and thanked the couple for allowing the unusual intrusion and led the shepherds out of the stable and into the night.

Many years later, Ezra kept his promise. He and his brother Simon shared the story of their encounter with the angels and looked for and found Jesus when He taught in their area as an adult. They followed Him and convinced many others to believe in Him as well. As a result, Ezra and Simon are in heaven with Jesus right now!

About Dr. Patty Sadallah

Patty Sadallah has a Doctorate of Ministry in Christian Leadership/Discipleship from Christian Leadership University. She is passionate about showing people how to encounter God personally so they may live their lives through faith in Jesus by the power of the Holy Spirit. Her mission is to bring the message of the realness of God and the practicality of intimacy and relationship with God to the masses by incorporating media in her messages.

Dr. Sadallah is a Professor at Christian Leadership University serving masters and doctoral students. Additionally, she leads the Spirit Life Circle mentored coaching ministry offered internationally through Communion with God Ministries.

She has more than 35 years' experience serving faith-based nonprofit organizations and small groups as an Organization Development Consultant, Coach, Facilitator, Trainer and Bible Study Leader.

Patty and George have been married since 1986 and have three lovely daughters: Jamael, Leah, and Noelle. Jamael and her husband Nick have their three sweet grandchildren.

Books by Dr. Patty Sadallah

Dr. Sadallah has authored the award-winning and recently updated book ***Clips that Move Mountains 2nd Edition,*** a Discipleship book which includes 23 film clips, and ***Journey to the Abundant Christian Life,*** its Bible study companion.

Additionally, ***How to Live a Worry-Free Life: Just ask Jesus Book 1.*** Look for more in this series after the completion of the Experience Jesus series.

The **Experience Jesus Series** includes 4 books

Book 1: *How to Encounter the LOVE of God; (Fall of 2020)*

Book 2: *How to Encounter the HEALING of God; (Winter 2020)*

Book 3: *How to Encounter the DIRECTION of God and (Spring 2021)*

Book 4: *How to Encounter the POWER of God. (Summer 2021)*

All books are available on **Amazon.com** and **BarnesAndNoble.com** The easiest way to find Dr. Sadallah's books is to **simply search "Patty Sadallah"** in these book store websites.

Check out more about each book and the other ministry opportunities by visiting her website at **www.PattySadallah.com**

Dr. Sadallah is available for speaking, teaching and facilitation related to discipleship for individuals, small groups, organizations, and multi-organizational planning needs.

God Bless you!

Patty Sadallah

CPSIA information can be obtained
at www.ICGtesting.com
Printed in the USA
LVHW081211210123
737580LV00008B/129